she's
gonna
be

she's
gonna
be

stories . poems . life
edited by Ann Decter

an all-girl production from
McGilligan Books

Canadian Cataloguing in Publication Data

Main entry under title:

She's gonna be : stories, poems, life

ISBN 0-9698064-6-9

1. Canadian literature (English) - Women authors .* 2. Lesbians' writings,
Canadian (English).* 3. Canadian literature (English) - 20th century.*
4. Women - Literary collections. 5. Lesbianism - Literary collections.
I. Decter, Ann, 1956 -

PS8235.W7S53 1998   C810.8'092871   C98-931500-2
PR9199.5.W6S53 1998

Credits -
"Walking Memories by the River" by Noreen Shanahan was previously
published in *Contemporary Verse 2*. "A Family Tree by Numbers" by
Ruth Mandel was previously published in *Fireweed*.

Editor: Ann Decter
Copy editor: Beth Pettigrew
Layout: Karen Woodman
Cover Illustration: Adapted from untitled #6 from *romantic notions* by Leah Decter
Cover Design: Sherree Clark
Interior Photographs: Sharon Baltman, Ann Decter
Proofreader: Noreen Shanahan

Contents

This Long Blossoming Spring

Women write desire, said the post-modern feminists, slashing faultlines in language through the 1980s. I'm furious, my mother raged through the '60s and '70s, as her generation's wave of feminism swelled and broke across the stubborn backsides of male chauvinist . . . remember? Pigs. A word for men. Fury, it was, sheer fury. It pulses now, too, here, more finely honed and with better access to the means of production. Sharp and specific.

Difference, intoned the feminist literary theorists, women write difference. Sometimes, we do. A different shape to emotions, different perspectives on the same event, different ambitions for our writing, sometimes. In her poem *Foot Frenzy*, Zoe Whittall writes revolution "with sparkles and cleavage and drill saws" seeking more than a satisfied ego and a spin on the lit world merry-go-round. In *A Family Tree by Numbers*, Ruth Mandel writes defiance of that "brand on unwilling skin", warning:

> That who I am
> must never be selected *(that word)*
> not for one split second
> not ever
> not on my life

Focus on difference views our written bodies as less determined and more determined by, existing in reference to – to borrow a line from poet and shero Joanne Arnott – "something huge, present and unnamed." To name it: that damnable patriarchy, and such a crappy word, too, for thousands of women's voices to raise in a chant – "No more patriarchy, no more shit!" – that doesn't catch until you round the slushy corner from Dundas onto Yonge and fling it viscerally at the tacky sex video parlours. "No more SHIT!" Configure that, literarily. Different, alright, to gaze from the street back to the sidewalk. Another way of seeing, another position to view the world from, newly-occupied spaces written into existence. The lesbian world that has come into visibility culturally in the last fifteen years, slips easily and unlabelled, into these pages, out of these women's lives.

While language theorists insisted our minds are inscribed by the philosophical and literary tattoo artists of Western Thought, from Plato to Shakespeare to Foucault – whose tools they picked up and ran with – a generation came of age inscribing their skin with abandon. Rebelliously celebrating their sexuality, they appropriate symbols and acts of the culture we are so different from – screaming electric guitar, S/M sexuality, kick-ass boots and even corporate commercialism – into a semantic space labelled "woman". This feminist generation plants its stakes of difference at least as often in opposition to constraining feminist orthodoxies as against a sweatless hogocracy.

This is a generation that writes where the previous one feared to tread. Once upon a time, not so long ago, a woman was not welcome to speak about suffering caused by other women. All suffering was caused by the "patriarchy", all violence attributed to maleness. Silence so religiously broken on other topics smothered women who lived violence perpetrated by women. All those admonitions to speak out were inapplicable. Now, women's violence is taken up by the mainstream, sensationalized, glamourized and offered as evidence of the inappropriateness of a feminist movement, because *voilà*, there is no *différence!* The embargo of the activist women's community has come to threaten support for shelters for assaulted women and children, to distort the actual frequency of violence initiated by women and camouflage the beauty of women's physical strength. While intoning "breaking the silence" into a cliché, we created our own. Here, it breaks. In this time, with the womanhood coming of age now.

Women write anger, yes, and desire. Women write trueness, words truly aimed and flying to the heart. Those clear, enchanting notes of the spirit. Women write potent realities, everyday cataclysms and hidden triumphs. Women write the quiet hunger of a refugee girl watching longshoremen load boats in occupied France, a fresh blast of winter infatuation tumbling into a bar for a quick scotch, feminestos and stalking stories, biker trips and buried babies.

I hear rhythm and cadence, feel the flow of life behind the writing in this collection. The calm assertion – she's gonna be – varied and alive, living anything and everything possible. Writing in relation to life, women structurally unmediated. Collapsing tired dichotomies of universality and domesticity. Execute a final, formal bow to the primacy of universality and it dissolves like sheer fabrication in the narrative power of particulars, the details of these lives we lead.

One night, as this long, blossoming spring gathered in the ground, I dreamed my way to somewhere like that woman's place of power Audre Lorde described — a place that is ancient, deep and dark. Brown as the earth that roots our being, soft as soil crumbling in my hand. Four women asleep on a bench in velvet silence. Each is wrapped in transparency, thin grey-blue, filigree tatters. They sleep on each other, pillowing bodies. I don't want to wake them, but I've come such a long way. And they are very hard to find. They are spectral, their ghostliness is the only light source. A fine, soft glow radiates as one moves. My mother. In the morning I will know she was with her friends, Dorothy, Carole and Niamh and realize they are women who populated my last novel. Now I know only that I must be quick, for my mother always loved to sleep and being dead so long, she must be that much more tired. It takes a lot to wake her. You must have something very interesting to say if you want to wake the dead. I stretch as big as I can, ten feet tall, rise and float above her. The bench is a porch swing, a swinging couch. My mother smiles up at me, that smile I came for, as I say, "I just wanted to show you how strong I've become."

"Yes, dear. I see," she answers. "How strong you are. Go ahead, now, and let us get back to our rest. We are with you. We are listening to your thoughts, we are waiting for the music of your writing to wake us."

Wake the muse, then, with the music of writing, out in fresher realms. Relegate silence to attics and basements, for silence can be death. Women write, provoking as often as accusing, taking quiet revenge and moving on, asserting new freedom, questioning philosophically. And laughing, on the page. That house I was born into, where the mind questions and inquires, observes and relates. Imagines. Where magic is a quality of mind, where a river of books carries a fluid discourse about life and living, in secret details and grand thoughts, in gestures and resolutions, in rages, tragedies and glittering, gut-busting irony. Where the mind has no gender. *She's Gonna Be* sits on those shelves, writing that joins in the great and boundless conversation conducted through books. For the sweetest core of life awaits in this simple technology bound together by a spine.

Ann Decter
Toronto, May 1998

"we will not be passive in our self-preservation"

Zoe Whittall

Karen Woodman

mph

Sherrie laughing, "I'm vain." Carmen tingling. It's still coursing through her. Difficulty with time. It's been ten fifteen this morning for too long. Speed injects heat into the bloodstream, battery acid. Awkward reflexes.

Driving through Davie Street listening to loud Erotic City. Their voices louder, telling each other how great they are. Tom says his mother told him he got the FREAK OF NATURE tattoo across his back because he has low self-esteem. He says he knows he's the greatest. The real me, MEET THE REAL ME. Sherrie driving. Everyone on the street looking grey. Carmen wearing lipstick, dark red lipstick, almost black. Slicked back hair with the good stuff that washes off, three coats of eyeliner, velvet pants and a long blue jacket with black velvet trim and motorcycle boots. A small metal gun and holster hang from her neck. Sherrie got it in Calgary. Sherrie says Carmen is on the prowl.

Speedball rollercoaster. One warm drop of sweat drips from Carmen's armpit down her side. No mood, no time for introspection at this moment. Speedball smoked with a ball point pen, a fine white chemical on a thin square of tinfoil. There is no hunger here. Speedball melt and one drop like a warm drop of sweat trickling, knowing but not feeling. Appendages warm and tingly, a thousand small shivers. Clarity. Clarity is relative. Speedball sweatdrip, it doesn't take much. Poetic interruption. External poetic interruption, is this fiction? Stratas of detachment, shock therapy without guilt or far-seeking ideals of morality. Indifference is the state between two strong emotions.

It took a long time to come down.

They felt cold again.

Downstairs into a room where Sherrie wants to dance. She doesn't know you. Long term things don't mean much to her anymore. Theatre assumes an audience. Sherrie says audiences are overrated. Horror sells well. Infatuation is the worst. It helps to fall asleep. Waking, possessions become things. Everyone changes.

Double scotch, Tom hiding in the background. Three years of cruising this place for a warm bed and whatever. No guilt, just doesn't want to be recognized. He knows the bartender and gets everyone free drinks. The bartender wonders what Tom is doing back here. Heard Tom moved to Toronto. Toronto was where it started. Tom leaves for the washroom. He takes a long time.

Sherrie the girl who burned down the schoolyard. The best pitcher. Overhand, fastball. Tomboy. Fucked in the lifeguard tower after dark. Coral blue room thirty feet off the ground. It was never locked. She was always breaking her wrists. Skinny at twelve, round by seventeen. Puke sick on rum red wine and tequila. Thirteen. Lying on her back pissed drunk in a park. The guy wanted her to suck his cock. She told him to fuck off. Her sister was murdered in Toronto. A man disguised as an electrician came to her apartment door and killed her. He already knew who she was. Young and beautiful. Sherrie liked to wear dark expensive sunglasses. She closed one eye and fluttered it when someone pissed her off.

Carmen with crushes on girls like Laura, with LAURA in bright yellow letters painted across the back of her LEE jean jacket and red DuMauriers and the taste of her cigarette in August. Carmen secretly sleeping with her new jean jacket for weeks.

The suburbs and mac jackets, jean jackets, tube tops, terry cloth ADIDAS shorts, foxy lady t-shirts, malls and shoplifting and waiting for buses. Carmen, Laura and Sherrie smoking in the skating rink shack and in comes Brown Owl wearing a toque scowling and saying it stinks in here and don't you girls have homework and Carmen, you've always had a bad attitude. That's your problem. Get out now. Then the little brownies skating in circles and trying to cut curves and falling backwards on bumpy ice. Gnomes, pixies, leprechauns and faeries helping people every day, especially those at home, singing Alice the camel has no humps, Alice the camel has no humps, Alice the camel has no humps cause Alice is a horse, tapping fingers softly on tightly woven industrial carpeting simulating the sound of rain and beating with open palms to imagine the sound of thunder. Rose, rose, rose, rose, will I ever see thee wed.

Sherrie and Carmen running through the back field chasing each other until shirts and jeans are off rolling and wet and sticky laughing and it never felt this good. Sherrie pregnant and the doctor at the free clinic downtown telling her she could get the abortion because she was still in high school. Carmen holding Sherrie's hand through automatic glass hospital doors.

Sherrie and Carmen, seven different GREYHOUND buses, three thousand miles and six to a room at the hotel on Main Street. Four months in Vancouver and five bucks goes a long way at the Ivanhoe where they meet Tom with a car and he wants to go dancing and you can't dance at the Ivanhoe. They just sit there and talk about how fucked up everything is in the world and Carmen thinks this is a bunch of shit because everybody knows it anyway. Let's go dancing and Sherrie knows speed has become important, so whatever happens it will be very soon. Carmen thinks they have traded one claustrophobia for another and her headaches are getting worse. She forgets to eat, hasn't called home in weeks, and it's ten fifteen.

Noreen Shanahan

December Roses

Rooted in –
my pluck unfolds twisted bulbs
unborn stems cling to raw bone-meal.

I lift your hand.
Demand you touch.
Then speak to you of death.

These smells, I say
tell of morbid dreams
rattlers snatch field mice
mewing lost and tail-less
along a maze of meadows.

Wait!
Lean closer to earth
it shudders, then roars
at our awakening.

Remember the rose
a single rose, curled
against Vancouver glass
that December.

Remember my excited voice
ripping through wires
tumbling towards Toronto.

Roses!
Christmas roses blooming!

Listen to the cadence in that, I say,
and dirty your hands with me now.

Elizabeth Ruth

Fat & the Fourth Dimension

Lunch was a 950 gram bag of rotini, boiled furiously and drowned in a tin of canned tomatoes. *The tomatoes were a definite mistake. Not good in reverse.* Lemon wiped her mouth along her sleeve. *No more evidence of lunch,* she thought. She had scoured the sink, opened the kitchen window to air out the room, and would soon change her shirt, washing it by hand. Lunch had also included three quarters of a double layer chocolate cake left over from her seventeenth birthday last Monday, four rows of saltines, and a plastic container of smoked salmon cream cheese. When she'd asked about the cheese in Kensington market, the man behind the counter offered her a taste. Lemon accepted the wafer with a glob of cheese twice its size, and allowed it to melt on her tongue religiously. She promised herself *if* she bought a small tin and *if* she ate only a bit each day it would be all right. Now, here she was, relieved again, leaning over the kitchen sink, empty of all will power. Filled with shame. Empty and full at once, trying to balance the leaking: those things she knows without being told. Things such as Jan's dad home drunk last night, loud and breaking glass, or a stranger crossing Bloor Street in rush hour and a minivan above the speed limit stopping him flat. Lunch took Lemon's mind off things, secrets she kept to herself. Lunch was a secret. One of the few things Lilith, her mother, didn't know about.

Lemon's face was red, her eyes swollen and watery. Her throat ached and although there was nothing more to regurgitate, it continued to contract. Lemon knew this was a bad sign. She was losing control. Used to be she filled and emptied herself infrequently, when she needed a distraction, like sorting the million papers inside her desk, or Ajaxing the bathroom, or having her hair cut just so. She liked to be organized, clean and prepared.

Lately, though, Lemon found herself heaving without deciding to, even without being full and most disturbingly, in public. Just the smell of an egg had sent her running to the washroom in the Eaton Centre last week. And the week before, it happened during the six o'clock news.

Peter Mansbridge really needs a hair piece, Lemon teased herself afterward, holding hands to eyes like a visor, squinting to protect against the imaginary glare off his forehead. But really, she was scared.

This morning in class, Lemon had fantasized about the cream cheese sitting on the second shelf behind the jug of orange juice, beside the milk. She had tried to push thoughts of it away, focus instead on her teacher, Mrs. Marsman who stood no more than four feet five inches above ground. Mrs. Marsman wore blazers over dress pants that appeared to shorten her stature even further, making it seem she had no legs anywhere. Mrs. Marsman's husband taught grade twelve chemistry. They smiled passing each other in hallways and at school assemblies, and when it was warm, they ate their lunch together outside. *Mmmm, lunch,* Lemon thought. *Just two hours left.*

Canadian history was a mandatory course and Lemon only ever remembered the insignificant highlights, like the fact that Eli . . . Eli somebody, Eli Whitney, invented the cotton gin, (actually, rumour had it his wife made the discovery) and this invention transformed something and was evidence of great ingenuity. Lemon thought Canada, like herself, was still trying to be something it wasn't by trimming away the heaviness: a legacy of colonialism, slavery and capitalism, and leaving a thin, hollow identity about which all that could be said was, we are not like America. *Well,* thought Lemon, looking at her size 16 thighs, *if Canada is not like America, then I am not like my mother.*

As Mrs. Marsman moved on to describe how, at one point in time, the east coast waters were overflowing with fish, Lemon could smell the salmon mixed into her cream cheese. She could. The cream cheese didn't just smell wonderful, it seduced her:

Pssst, Lemon, you there?

Go away.

Lemon, you hungry?

Shut up. It's only ten in the morning.

You want me, you know you do.

I don't.

You can't say `no' to me.

`No.' There, I said it.

But you don't mean it.

Yes I do.

Who are you kiddin'?

We both know what's gonna happen when you get home.

No we don't.

Oh yeah? What happened yesterday?

That was different.

How?

Yesterday was a bad day. It was dark and drizzly, I forgot my wallet and had to walk to class and then Jan wasn't around because she stayed home sick.

O.K. Yesterday sucked. But you know what?

What?

Today's gonna suck too.

Leak — Then, Lemon drifted forward into another dimension as Mrs. Marsman continued her lecture.

It was International Women's Day, well into the new millennium. Year 2015, perhaps. Lilith was sitting in the sound booth of a campus radio station.

"You've got to be big," Lilith said.

"Could you explain that statement on air, Ms. Boot? It's just the kind of message we want our young listeners to absorb."

"Call me Lilith, honey."

"Ok." The interviewer shuffled some papers, scribbled notes down the margins, and nodded at the woman on the other side of the glass. A red light turned green, signalling the show had begun.

"The statistics are alarming! Almost ninety-five percent of anorexics and bulimics are women. Up to twenty percent of female college students are actively bulimic. Dieting has become pandemic, and most women attempt to lose weight regardless of body type. As women enter the workforce, pressure to conform multiplies. The good news is we are better educated than ever before. We can resist the pressure. One way to do that is to draw upon the experiences of other women. Today in the studio, we are fortunate to be joined by several professional women who will discuss the impact body size has had on their self-esteem and jobs. Ms. Boot, we'll begin with you: Could you comment on the relationship between your work and your size?

"Come again?"

"Have you found yourself treated unjustly, perhaps even discriminated against in employment situations, as a result of being a large woman?"

"Honey, I'm not large. Large is how you might describe a four-by-four or a skyscraper. I'm fat."

"Yes, well, some women choose to identify as f-f-f-fat, while others prefer large or Rubinesque. Nevertheless, many women support the claim that a woman's body size can be linked to her economic status. After all, how many images of large women succeeding in high profile professions do we find in magazines and on television?"

"You girls are too hung up on money if you ask me."

"F-f-f-further evidence to support women's claims of fat oppression can be found in the famous quote, `a woman can never be too rich or too thin'."

"Real hung up. There's more to li-"

"And . . . uh, women receive socio-cultural messages that being thin is equivalent to success in employment situations. Has that, um, has that ever happened to you, Ms. Boot?"

"Never."

"Are you certain?"

"Yeah."

"So, are you saying that as a large woman in a society that worships thinness, you have never been adversely affected by unrealistic beauty ideals?"

"Not that I remember."

"Perhaps then, you could explain for our listeners how you have become immune to such pressure? Ms. Boot, what's the cure for the stigma or sizeism?"

"There's nothin' medical about it," Lilith said.

The interviewer rolled her eyes at the production assistant.

"It's just better to be big. Besides, I like to eat, fast food mostly. My daughter says I eat so many preservatives *I* probably have a shelf life of a hundred years."

"Ms. Boot, would you mind telling our listeners what profession you are in?"

"Sure, honey, I'm a clairvoyant."

The interviewer threw her hands into the air, papers scattered across the table. "You mean you are a psychic."

"I prefer clairvoyant." Lilith winked at the interviewer.

"Fine. As a clairvoyant, you have found being fat has worked to your advantage?"

"Now we're getting somewhere."

"Could you explain that?"

"Being a clairvoyant is about time and space. The bigger I am, the wider my reach, you might say. It's simple: the more of me there is, the more I can see; like you see things as three dimensional, but I see into the fourth."

The room was silent. Dead air. The green light began to flicker red.

"Our time is just about up for this segment," the interviewer said. "I would like to thank our first guest for taking time out of her busy schedule to provide an alternative perspective on women and weight preoccupation. Perhaps Ms. Boot will return another time to continue the discourse on fat and the fourth dimension."

Lilith smiled widely.

"Lemon Boot!" Mrs. Marsman called.

Lemon hadn't heard the question.

"Try to stay with the rest of the class, dear."

"Um, Mrs. Marsman?"

"Yes."

"I'm not feeling well. I think I'd better go home."

Excerpt from the novel, Leaking.

Zoe Whittall

Foot Frenzy

At 9, I wanted suede ankle boots
pointy like the Solid Gold dancers
my mother said I'd look like a streetwalker
and got me the grey velcro sneakers
with the baby-bonus cheque
I ripped them open and closed real fast
hoping to age them
painted them pink to match my jean skirt
It was no use explaining to my mom that
pointy-toed shoes were a playground privilege
catty girls could taunt the boys
threats of kicking them where it hurts
with wicked shoe weaponry
In my headphones Janet Jackson sang
      "Nasty boys . . . don't mean a thing."

At 16, I wanted 6-hole cherry docs
with colour-coded anti-racist laces
allowance and baby-sitting bills
stuffed in empty beer bottles
we smashed on the sidewalk
to buy doc martens
real punk girls were made with
wool socks in ankle boots
that said, I'm no fucking cheerleader
I can stomp by and ignore you
journals filled with
no-one-understands me poetry
in my headphones Courtney Love sang
      "I'm Miss World, somebody kill me."

At 17, I wanted thrift store combat boots
duct-taped in art college
we will not be passive
in our self-preservation
we will not dress to impress
just to be a real woman
there is no lady in the nails
digging through my heels
in my headphones Ani Difranco sang
       "I'm determined to survive on this shore,
       you know I don't avert my eyes anymore."

At 21, I wanted bitch diesel platforms
we stand and command
in twirl and girl motion
a parade of positive possibility
a step in a sexy direction
reclaiming feminine protection
with sparkles and cleavage and drill saws
no need to run in stilettos
'cause walking real slow keeps the gaze on
and the power in your confident posture
in my headphones, 7 Year Bitch sang
       "Silence is defeat"

mariko tamaki

Burt Reynolds

Last nite I had this sex dream where I was about to have sex with this redneck old guy I was baby-sitting for when we realized he didn't have a condom.

It was so heart-breaking.

We were just in the middle of this crazy carnival make-out session when it dawned on me that we were about to have sex and I got all excited.

"Okay, let's go," I said. "Do you have a condom?"

Right away he gets all tense.

"Why," he says, like he's in some public service announcement, "do you think I have AIDS or something?"

"No," I said, "but, as you know, it certainly isn't worth taking the risk."

I could see he was getting upset.

"Plus there's birth control and other sexually transmitted diseases to consider."

I was beginning to get a little turned off. I mean, really, who did this dude think he was? Even if he was really cute and looked, with his mustache, a little like my grade seven science teacher, he certainly wasn't TO DIE FOR. I was beginning to wonder just how many of his baby-sitters ended up in the sack with him (never mind the fact that I was supposed to be baby-sitting and I had NO IDEA where the kids were). Still, I really wanted to have sex.

I think I even offered to go and buy a condom but he was super agitated and started this big c'mon-why-don't-we-just-get-it-*on* speech.

Halfway through he said, "You know, this is a dream. I don't think you can get AIDS if you have sex without a condom in a dream."

Like that's the point.

"Still," I reasoned, "it's symbolic."

Men.

What a panty twister. I was so mad I insisted he pay me double for my baby-sitting time and fork over an extra ten for a cab. I think I may have had sex with the cab driver on the way home, out of pure desperation.

If I recall, HE had a condom, and looked a little like Burt Reynolds.

Monica Noy

Dust

In my memories history has not been made, but lingers like summers that lasted forever, bare feet dancing over hot roads and gravel driveways. My hands betray; the weather has taken its toll on them, the past sucks the elasticity out of my skin with its relentless passing. The lines, and the bones, are the only evidence of the childhood I have waited thirty-five years to out grow. I was blinded by a ruse that wrapped my mind in a membrane of nostalgia and fled my body.

Since the day she left, like a mirage drifting up from melting asphalt, I have scrambled for her past, clutched onto my own. The corners of recollection remain as she left them, filled with dust motes and errant food scraps. I did not dare clean, in case something was lost. Waiting all this time for her to come back to the child I was that day, squashing flies in the summer heat, waiting for her to make me wash my hands, wash the dishes, go to bed. These things she did by rote, never checking if my hands were clean, or if I was asleep, but she did them nevertheless, like a religion, or a mantra of motherhood; words I came to rely on, actions I came to trust. When she left she took that trust with her. Like a child asleep in the back of a car, I have longed for that security. An adult now able to drive, I have never been able to regain it.

Her leaving was like death, permanent. Though her ghost came back to haunt us, and the secret to haunt her. The decomposed bones of a long buried skeleton, resolution vanishing with the flesh that once adorned it.

Mother is the only one who knows the whole story, the only one who ever did. I know some of it, but it's been so long, and so many have died while I waited, afraid, mourning the babies that never were. The baby I never was, and she never had.

Only Uncle Laurel dusted. Dusted, cleaned and shelved secrets like they were fine china, locked them inside a wooden cabinet so the children could not touch. From the very beginning (and I do not know where that is) he hid the dirt under a carpet and kept the polished silver mysteries locked away, right here at the farm.

I loved this place, the place of the waterfall. A gentle baptism of dewy rainbows or an icy stream of fast-moving glass. A mere trickle during times of drought, which seemed more common than not. One year it didn't flow at all, not a drop to wet the desperate moss, peeling from the rocks. Even city dwellers had to watch lawns and flowers die in the venting sun, forbidden by law to offer even the tiniest drop of sustenance. Some people watered of course, but only when the street lamps were about to flicker off and sweaty bodies slumbered fitfully under sheets of humidity. That year the tanks almost dried up at the farm, and all over the surrounding countryside. That year the fields were yellow, and the dog lost her leg in a tractor accident. I was there. I watched Uncle Laurel and Uncle Harding struggle through. We banded together, the three of us in the dust. I, too young and transient to do much more than watch them bake in the sun with their land, becoming like it; tough, leathery and resilient. That was so long ago. Harding used to say, "There's a good sweat and a bad sweat, and when you're working, you're sweating the good sweat." I was sweating the good sweat, we all were, drinking in the sun just the same as if it had been the cool trickle of the waterfall.

Laurel's been dead these past two years, and Harding close to twenty. Both contracted cancer, passing it on like a contagious disease. Harding slipped quickly, before he even had time to be sick he was dead. But not Laurel, he and that cancer hung onto each other in a grim parody of a symbiotic relationship. I still don't understand why he kept breathing so long. He died long before his heart stopped beating, on the same day as Harding, when he became an empty shell of a man working a farm that no longer meant anything to him. Except, maybe, for the skeleton. He knew I'd find it eventually. That's why he left the place to me when he died. Why he left me the key. He wanted me to find it, wanted me to wipe the cobwebs away and dust the corners. Laurel stopped cleaning the day Harding died, but he couldn't let me begin, not while he was still alive.

I searched his once-tidy little world, climbing on chairs to reach the very top shelf. There were things to be found. Photographs; well-kept secrets. I asked him about them, kicked drying clods of dirt into his clean recesses. He wouldn't budge. His words took shape behind opaque glass, quandaries I am guessing at still.

Charlie lies asleep on the bed opposite me. Charlie fills me, has always filled me; from the moment of conception to the moment of her

birth, she has been a scent, a banquet. She is concentrated joy, uncondi-
tional love. She is oxygen and water. She is food and shelter. I am the
mother I always wanted to have. I am larger than life.

Her lashes flutter in sleep, the delicate tickle of spider's feet on her
cheek; they are a gift from her father, though her green eyes were once
mine. I gave them freely, wanted her to see what I have seen, the way I
have seen it. Wanted her to understand how things happened, so she
could one day find the pieces of the puzzle that are missing. Her father is
outside, enjoying the cool breeze of a warm summer evening with people
he only just met. Australians who, when they've sucked back a few cold
ones, will talk the ear off his poor Canadian head. He'll understand some
of it, clues revealed by my colloquial way of talking; when we first met I
had such misplaced pride in my country and its language. It wasn't long
before I began to call the toilet a washroom, and say excuse me and sorry
with such frequency, such commonality.

There is an uproar outside. Mocking laughter; the sound of a hit
reaching its bull's-eye. I bet the target is Nathaniel. Some joker probably
asked him to "pass the dead 'orse" so they could drown their burned
chop in it. Nathaniel doesn't even call it tomato sauce, he calls it ketchup.
I warned him, told him not to believe a thing any of them said. Australian's are famous for "taking the piss." Sarcasm is a way of life here, a castle
wall and a piranha-filled moat. Only the very brave dare to push through.
Nathaniel doesn't have that barrier, it was too easy to fall into him. When
I beat at him, expecting it to be there, he flinched. Eventually I packed
the battering ram away, but coming back has brought it out again, along
with the defences, like pushing a button; boom, an impenetrable wall.

Shadows prostrate themselves across the vast tracts of land that once
belonged to me, and a single beam of light struggles to illuminate the
room. It splashes through the small window above the door and plays on
the ceiling. It won't be there for long, but while it is I can see what is in
the small chest. I have come full circle. But it is not a perfect circle, the
beginning doesn't quite hook up to the end. I am close enough.

Looking down at the pieces that remain in the little chest, so like a
casket, I wonder how much of her is like me, and me like her. So small,
the misshapen skull rolls around in the palm of my hand, the eye sockets
elongated. There are no teeth. There are some other bones, or parts thereof,
in the casket, too. What might have been a leg bone, a rib bone, part of
the spinal column. She is reduced to bare essentials. Life bleached from

her by time, the great healer of all wounds. Yet, even in such death, she has a voice. Her bones click together as I put them gently back into the chest, joining the laughter coming from outside.

I look up at the ceiling, drenched with a glow from the floodlights, nowhere near as strong as the sun. I can no longer see inside the chest and it is a comfort, not to be able to see her, hear her, though I am the last person she will ever talk to. Her sister. She does not even have a name.

If I call her Pandora then I must be the keeper of her secret.

I will do what my mother never got the chance to, what Laurel could not bear to. I will crush the bones to fine dust and throw them to the wind. I will burn the photographs and bury the ashes. I will tell my mother in so many words, ashes to ashes, dust to dust. I will end it here.

What could I tell Charlie anyway? How could I put together a story from the disjointed pieces of information I have gained? There is nothing conclusive, nothing concrete to go on. I have missed so many clues. The ones I have lead nowhere, simply more questions to be asked, more clues to be found. It is too late now, mouths are rotted with sweet conundrums, stories pasted onto the paltry information that remains. I am left with fragments of a truth which has no context, left with only lies. I have tried to fill in the gaps surrounding us; the children who have lived and died. Of my success I cannot say, it depends on the view. I have, at best, a palimpsest thrice erased and begun again. Smeared chalk turns the blackboard grey and I am unable to read between the lines to find the original story.

It is time to dust.

Prologue to the novel, The Meadowlea Mum

Shlomit Segal

Conversa

Ana has gone to see the rabbi
to learn about being a Jew
since her family cannot tell her –
they only know Easter, communion, patron saints

I see her in his study
leatherbound tomes line his bookshelves
Torah, Talmud, Gemara

the rabbi plays with his glasses
describes kashrut, mitzvot, shabbat
the Ashkenazi rules

Ana, with long curls
black as a raven
twirls a lock
around her index finger
Ana, lily among the thorns
re-crosses her legs
in stylish dark tights

Ana is a phenomenon
her Portuguese accent is slight
she recounts stories of
candles in the cellar
whispers in the village
strange symbols on her grandfather's books
back in the Azores

she has never heard the words
converso, marrano, crypto-Jew
she just knows Judeo
spit out like a curse

    Ana, there is a skylight
    you can see in
    if you crouch on the roof

    Let's rise above those glass cases
    of rabbinic writings
    and charity awards
    in the conservative shul

    Let's follow the path
    that leads to the edge of the woods
    to the gathering place
    the kitchen, the candles,
    the stories, the forest

    Maybe we can find what was lost in 1492:
    love poems
    and almond cookies
    medical studies and guttaral songs
    the coasts of Sepharad
    where our ancestors gathered
    under domed rooves
    until sparks lit up the sky

I see her reading Yehuda Halevy and Judith Plaskow
going back to find that book
inscribed with aleph and bet

I see her in a union meeting
wearing the magen david on a chain
or with her new lover
drinking wine on shabbat
leading services
wrapped in a rainbow talit
at a lecture about the Middle East

Ana, this is also Jewish
this patchwork of hearts
that proclaims: never again
never anyone

this spirit that stands on one foot
instead of building fences
this community that says kaddish
in a circle of extended arms

hands that carry banners
feed friends with hearty soup
these women and men
who continue to carry out the work
though it is not upon us
to complete the task.

Glossary

aleph and bet - first two letters of the Hebrew alphabet
Ashkenazi - central and Eastern European Jews
converso/a, marrano, crypto-Jew - Jews who converted to Christianity during the Spanish inquisition, but secretly practiced Judaism. Marrano is derogatory.
gemara - Jewish religious text
kaddish - prayer for the dead
kashrut - keeping kosher, Jewish dietary laws
magen david - Star of David
mitzvot - religious commandments or good deeds
Judith Plaskow - Jewish feminist theologian
Sepharad - Spain in Hebrew
shabbat - the sabbath, sunset Friday to sunset Saturday
shul - Yiddish for synogogue
talit - prayer shawl
torah - the first five books of the Jewish bible
talmud - Jewish religious text
Yehuda Halevy - famous poet of Jewish golden era in Spain

Ruth Mandel

A Family Tree by Numbers

If the concentration camps had been liberated in 1943 or 1944
I could have done my family tree
by numbers.
Now only one such branch, Auschwitz-Birkenau 6 4 1 8 9,
(my great aunt Erna)
still smoulders from the brand
against unwilling skin.

My uncle Henryk is the child
neighbours promised to protect.
They threw him onto the street,
denounced him at the age of nine,
they kicked him and kicked him.
And I am told that my grandmother
knew in a dream from her hiding place
that he was made to bleed to death slowly
on the street.

My grandmother Henia finds her grave
softer now
on the branch that is my middle name.
And same too
my great-grandmother Ruth
about whom I can know almost nothing.

My father Roman (Raymond now)
a small child then,
receives *reparations payments* from the German government.
In spite of his fear, he has grafted
three children to absent bark.
In spite of the flames stalking him,
searing his offspring,
transferring the genetically coded
Warning

that who I am
must never be decided
by uninvited courts

Warning
That who I am
must never be selected *(that word)*
not for one split second
not ever
not on my life

That if ever I am only a Jew to a Nazi
only a woman to a man
only a soldier to an army
only an obstacle to a bullet

If ever I am only
a number or a name

Then surely
    I am
    on fire
    again.

Ruth Mandel

Old Boxes

"I'm German" she blurts, as I emerge from the bathroom stall
after reading my holocaust poetry at this women's writing retreat.
She is tall, blond, somewhat gangly, leaning a little too close
and clearly has more to tell me.
"My dad was in Hitler Youth, but I can't ask him about it.
His parents enrolled him. Sometimes I think my grandparents
say anti-semitic things, but I'm not sure and I can't
ask them about it either."

What am I supposed to say? Evidently
this is a disclosure for her. But, really,
who ever wants to hear about another anti-semite?

She continues "We don't talk about it."

"That's hard in a family."

"Yes" she sighs.

"Well, if you can't talk about it in your family,
it's good to find others to talk with" I say warily.

"I thought you might know about Hitler Youth,
the kinds of things they did, that my father
might have done, I sort of think it was like Scouts."

"No, it wasn't like Scouts, no."

"You don't think so?"

Fucking oppressors, their kids
grow up wide-eyed and naive,
while victims' kids are born twinned
to suffering and danger.
"There are lots of books on the subject. But
why don't you just ask your father. Books won't tell you
exactly what *he* did."

"I could never ask him. No way. It would be too uncomfortable."

"Well, you just asked me. And it made me uncomfortable.
Why should *I* be uncomfortable and not your father?"

"But you're used to talking about it."

"No, it's miserable and wretched every time.
I just have no choice. I can't pretend nobody was murdered.
Believe me, I'd rather have been born into one of those
cheerful, crowded, cousin-upon-cousin families
who have great big reunions with signs
posted along country roads to get everybody to the right party."

"I think my grandparents might still be anti-semitic" she repeats
in a manner so self-conscious that she seems, ironically,
to be perpetuating a silence
rather than breaking it. Complicit.

"Why defend *them?* Why not *me?*
Me. I'm who they're talking about. Doesn't that bug you?
Don't you think you should call them on it?"

"It wouldn't feel right" she answers, too quickly.

"Oh yes it would. At least, it would *be* right.
Why not argue, make them feel a bit crummy,
tell them straight out they are wrong.
I know it's hard, who wants to upset their grandparents?"
Fuck 'em. Shake 'em up.
Don't let them go about with their deadly beliefs.
Make them pay. Make them change.

She reverses direction "I don't really mind
not knowing the details. I mean we get along well, y' know?"

"I'm sure you do. It works well for everybody. If nobody
asks questions, nobody has to answer them."
How dare you unleash
this wicked subject and then scramble away?
Afraid of a little conflict? You won't rile your father
or your grandparents, but you will rile me?
"I don't have an easy time of it, why should you?
Anyway, why ask *me*, of all people,
to answer for *them*? It's obscene, don't you think? I won't
make it easy for you. It's not like me
to let anybody off the hook."

"Well I doubt they did anything, anything
really bad" she says nervously.

"What was bad, really *bad, bad enough*, what was *good*?
It's not the point. I'm sure it's taking a lot of courage
for you to talk, but what do you want from *me*? Forgiveness
for not challenging your family? Absolution for them?
It's your past, *you* take responsibility for it.
Don't shove it over to me."

She lets it sink in "I don't think they really want me to know."

"Yah, but do *you* want to know? That's really the question.
You have to go from there. Think about it at least,
why do I have to stir things up and not you? Why do I dig up
my family's stories and you let yours
be buried? Afraid of what you might find out?"

What would German children find
if they reached into the back of the family's cupboards,
poked about in the deep drawers?
An old box?
Old photos   old uniforms   old beliefs   old
murders
their family did not
prevent.
I wash my hands, dry them on my jeans.
We walk out of the washroom.
I relent
"You got your hand slapped once, eh."

She nods.

"Been there" I bridge

Sharon Baltman

Biker Trail

Overlooking the Smoky Mountains in Gatlinburg, Tennessee. I'm alone in a woody chalet. Five HARLEY-DAVIDSON motorcycles drip impotently in the teeming rain. The familiar red Decker with its rear license plate, *HUZR*. Yiddish for pig, the mascot of HARLEY riders. The wraparound windshield with triple proboscis fronts black vinyl LAZ-Y-BOY seats. The rear one will be my perch for the next five days. Steely chrome glints between raindrops. Chunky saddle bags drape the back wheel which is topped by a deep red metal bucket. On this storage box sits a rear-facing, soggy, twelve-inch stuffed pink pig with black leather cap. Out of the darkness, an enormous chair-lift lumbers up the mountain in front of me, beyond the chalet balcony. Where am I, I wonder, gazing into the looming blackness. When my five biker friends left Toronto to ride down to Tennessee, I was in Mont Tremblant, visiting my daughter at summer camp. I flew down to meet them and tour the Smoky Mountains, and ride back with them through the Northeastern United States.

Because of the rain, my friends couldn't pick me up at the Knoxville airport as planned. Instead, Carrie Gayle brought me here in her limo from the airport. A hip, young-looking Black grandmother, she chatted warmly as we drove. "I've driven cab for two years now, and I've learned all the tricks of the trade. I work when I want, and I like to drive nice and slow and carefully. I had a good job with the Marriott food division at the University of Chattanooga. Good job, but I prefer drivin' cab. That's Dollywood over there, the extravaganza tourist site that Dolly Parton set up where she was born, so we don't ever forget her and her music." Carrie Gayle laughed out loud at my amazement with the tackiness of the area. We crawled through Pigeon Forge, capital of the Smokies, with wide stretched-out streets, single-storey outlets lining both sides and generous green boulevards running down the centre. Gaudy signs hawked wedding chapel services. Garish billboards touted every tiny bric-a-brac shop.

Crowds swarmed, even in the rain. Bumper stickers read: "I support Pro Life." License plates from Mississippi, Alabama, Manitoba. We were in Tourist Alley, family playland of Middle America.

Where am I, I wondered again. It was Tuesday, July 30th, therefore:

If it was 8 a.m., I was in Toronto.

If it was 10 a.m., I was in New York City.

If it was 1 p.m., I was in Nashville, Tennessee.

If it was 6 p.m., I was in Knoxville.

If it was 8 p.m., I was in Gatlinburg.

I was starving. There was nothing to eat in the chalet. My friends had gone grocery shopping. Grey plastic airplane food had never appealed to me. My only meal all day had been in the white table-clothed dining room in the Nashville airport. A teased-blonde southern belle encouraged, "Go for the grilled veggie kebab, honey. It's way betta than the deep-fried catfish, or Tennessee Bar-B-Q. That ain't nuthin' but a plain ole shredded pork sandwich." A colourful plate of black-striped fresh vegetables arrived, garnished with a flowing honey-mustard dressing. She treated me to local brewed iced tea served in a bottomless clear glass pitcher, loaded with sparkling cubes. The southern belle told me to finish with southern chocolate pecan pie. This was not a drizzle of chocolate on top of pecan pie, but a layer of creamy, chocolatey, nutty syrup beneath a roof of crunchy giant pecans, with a white melt of ice cream turning chocolate on the plate. Sated, I wandered through the airport and picked up my only other Nashville souvenir - a blue plastic fly-swatter in the shape of a guitar. The perfect gift for Henry, a lover of knick-knacks, who'd be riding the red Decker, *HUZR*, with me.

The rain continued for two days, so we ate, for two days. Rob, the enormous trip organizer, loved his steak and lobster.

"Cook me up those carrots, eh," he barked at me. Persistent orange firmness caused bubbling resentment to rise from the hot tub to meet the cool raindrops later that night.

"Damn women always make trouble. Shouldn't take them on long trips like this," Rob grumbled, as the rain continued. And as the days passed, he was more insistent that things be done his way. He demanded we use limbs and umbrellas as safer transport into town — rather than wheels and rainsuits. He refused to dine out, and chose hearty meat and potatoes over vegetarian fare that others preferred.

The sun finally emerged on the third day, but Dawn's starter failed, and our battery was dead. Our first destination was the closest HARLEY-DAVIDSON dealership, in the suburbs of Knoxville. We spent the day there. All day. A huge shop, with racks and racks of HARLEY products: T-shirts – large and small, bustiers – stretchy and skimpy, hats – baseball and bandanna, leathers – adults' and children's, sunglasses – raunchy and tame. Two things in common: logo, and price. Rock music pumped. Big Rob wandered impatiently. Henry, shorter, but only slightly smaller in girth, ran next-door for banana cream pie. Dawn and I chatted in the warm sunshine, away from the revving engines. I concluded that HARLEYS were designed to break down easily, so their owners had nothing to do but shop while the bikes were being fixed. I, too, succumbed. I bought myself a purple T-shirt. In a child's size, not much smaller than the adult's, and much cheaper. Finally, the bikes were on the road. That first day, we only had enough time to check out a couple of chintzy tourist shops in Gatlinburg, the "Queen of Garish", and go for dinner.

The rain had robbed us of touring time, and before we knew it, we had only one day left to tour the Smokies before heading toward home. In the early morning light, we dressed in layers. Although it was midsummer, we were high in the mountains, and at eighty kilometres an hour, there would be a major chill. My jeans and T-shirt were followed by a green wool turtleneck. I donned leather boots over woolly socks. Then came the ubiquitous black leather – mine without H.D. logo – jacket, scarf, gloves, and, of course, leather chaps. The original cowgirl. I learned to fit my unruly locks into the helmet, braiding them into two pigtails that I encased in rust suede wraps bought in the "Cherokee" store. (These shops were an annoying American tourist invention. They supposedly sold cottage industry products to generate revenue for local Indigenous people. So why were all the employees white, and had no clue how the products were made, where they came from, nor what their use was?) My head was crowned by the hard, hot, heavy, headache-engendering helmet. The "boys" packed the necessary gear onto the bikes. Every item in its place. Every bungee cord wrapped securely. Never enough bungee cords. They fussed like fathers over newborn sons. We had been living in order to ride. Now, we would "Ride to Live." Five loaded glistening bikes thundered up the hill, carrying six bobbing helmets.

The roar of the engines imprints on your brain. Contact with the world is complete. What surrounds you, envelops you. The air is cold on your face. Your body is not cold. You smell the fresh morning dew. Feel it on your cheeks. Watch its wetness rise off the green fields around you. You ride down one hill into the mist, up out of it on another. The haze clears. The sky is your leader. If it's blue, you're free. If it's cloudy, you've got to think. Tall trees whiz by, cast the aromas of pine, fir, and fungus. Untasted from a car, the pungent smell of sweetgrass comes and goes. It is pure ecstasy.

As the sun rose, we lined up at the roadside to remove a layer at a time. We rode through the mountains, watched deer graze beside the road. We pulled over to behold valleys of green. Crisp air cleaned our lungs. We vroomed through old wooden covered bridges. As we geared down to take another blind corner in the Smoky Mountains, the throaty groan of the HARLEY pierced the calm. We sailed along a portion of the famous Blue Ridge Parkway, with manicured fields, dense forests and rolling vistas. We roared through quiet pastoral scenes of fenced corrals, lazy cows, and white-painted barns.

Mostly we travelled the scenic routes. I had the cushioned high-back seat with armrests on the rear of the Decker, the large touring HARLEY. The stereo blared The Three Tenors, alternating with the local rock station. When our route forced us onto congested, fast-paced, and boring throughways, I fell asleep. I managed to hang on to the side-handles, and save my eye-power for the interesting stuff.

We tried to ride close together, to be aware if anyone was in distress. It also helped keep those of us with no sense of direction on the correct route. Two days into our homeward journey, just inside West Virginia, we suddenly noticed that we were only four. One of the bikes was no longer with us. We doubled back about three kilometres to find Derek's silent bike deserted at the roadside in the setting sun. We found Derek jabbering on the phone in a nearby farmhouse, trying to find a HARLEY dealer to check out his dead bike. He arranged a tow for the next day. Big Rob decided he would wait around with Derek for the repair, and ordered the rest of us to go on home. Derek had bought his lemon from Rob only six months earlier. "We can finally relax," said Dawn, who'd been repeatedly chastised by Rob, including the time she got an ice cream when she had only stopped to pee.

We overnighted at inexpensive roadside motels willing to book bikers. One night was spent in Lewisburg, West Virginia. We pulled in after dark, and had drinks in a bar with six other HARLEY riders, talking bikes. Next morning we toured the Sharp General Store (since 1884) in Slatyfork, West Virginia, the middle of nowhere. Original high ceilings, old wooden counters, glass display cabinets, antique cash registers, and vintage products of a general store. A mannequin stood behind the counter, clad only in a mink boa. "Modern amenities sold, too." The next night was in Kittaning, Pennsylvania. Highlight was breakfast the next morning at J.J.'s Home-Cooking in Bellwood, Pennsylvania, fourth of July stars and stripes still hanging on the fourth of August. A greasy-spoon diner from a movie set. For a very small price, we downed endless warm, toasted L.A. Cinnamon Bread dripping with butter.

Because we had many miles to ride in a short period of time, we blazed through a Victorian town of two-storey board and batten row houses along a main street, lace curtains, stained glass windows, and quaint shops. We passed through so quickly, I don't know whether it was Beallsville, Brownsville or Blairsville, Pennsylvania. We covered a lot of pavement in three days, and by the third night, we were back in Toronto.

I thought I had passed through my adult life without addiction. This trip taught me I was wrong. Five days on a HARLEY was intoxicating. While I didn't undergo withdrawal when I split from the bike's owner, I still craved the HARLEY's vibrations. The appeal of the owner melted away, but my love of the HARLEY stands firm, and threatens me with addiction. I learned the true meaning of the expression that lured the early explorers: "It's the voyage, not the destination."

Mehri Yalfani

Happiness in Five Definitions

It was Bahman who initiated the discussion about happiness. The night, the moonlight, the forest, the silence, the fire which flamed occasionally, spreading a pleasant heat, the glory of nature, so rich and deep, might have been the reason that Bahman, who had been thinking about happiness for a long time, posed his question, and raised a lot of discussion. But, also, he was a questioning person, eager to know everybody's definition of life and happiness. Bahman collected booklets, asked everyone their ideas about everything. He had read and heard many definitions and still at any gathering, he posed a question when something came to mind. They were sitting around a fire in a provincial campground. Three tents in different colours and sizes close by, the children asleep in them. Bahman hadn't married yet and didn't have any children. Perhaps because of that he liked to busy himself posing questions to friends and companions, seeking answers on every aspect of life.

Hamed was always interested in Bahman's questions and definitions. He was the first to volunteer an answer. Not only did Hamed consider himself a happy man, others had no doubt that he deserved to be happy. He had a good education: a Ph.D. in mathematics, which meant he was perfectly logical in the conception of his life, no doubts, illusions or mirages. A Ph.D. in mathematics meant he was a man of action with a good job, a good salary, and most importantly, his job was secure. Many organizations who sought intelligence looked to him. Hamed had a good wife, obedient, loyal, receptive and subordinate to him. He had good children, gifted and well-nourished, without any sign of problems in school. So, Hamed deserved to be happy. He was aware of, and proud of, his happiness.

"What does happiness mean, in your opinion?" Bahman asked.

Hamed had his answer ready. First, he looked around, to be sure everyone was interested. A sarcastic smile made him appear pleased with himself. The fire flared again as Bahman added dry wood.

"I wish you had posed a more complicated question," Hamed said, "happiness has a simple definition."

Abdolah, a man of defeated actions, bankrupt businesses, and fruit-less works, a disappointed man of hard work which yielded no fruit, who liked to make a joke out of any serious job, who always had a sneer rather than a smile, looked at Hamed. Abdolah sometimes confused a sneer and a smile. He believed there was no seriousness left in life. Everything looked like a comic play since he had been uprooted from his homeland and thrown faraway. Serious things had become jokes. Abdolah looked at Hamed and said, "The most simple definition might be the most com-plex to explain. For example, aging, it's so simple, everybody can feel it everyday, fatigue in your body and wrinkles in your face in the mirror. This simple phenomena relates to the whole universe. If you want to learn about it, you need to study the milky way and black holes and the solar system. Because the whole universe is aging with you."

Hamed was annoyed with Abdolah's habit of commenting on every single word coming out of everybody's mouth, especially Hamed's, who had been interrupted several times that day. He said impatiently, "I have nothing to do with the whole universe. I would like to give you a simple definition of happiness. Isn't that clear?"

Homa admired Hamed silently, as she had all her life, like a dog admiring her master, even when he does nothing. She looked at Abdolah, offended that he had interrupted Hamed again. She cursed Abdolah quietly. Homa believed Hamed was the most important person among men, and more so among men and women, because women were no-body.

Hamed scrutinized everybody with a hurt look on his face, waiting for Bahman to insist on his answer. Bahman waited for Hamed's answer. Manijeh pushed the half-burned wood into the fire, a vague smile in her face. She was a learned woman. Manijeh had many definitions for social and spiritual concepts. She was part philosophical thinker. She knew many names of philosophers, and sometimes liked to mention their names as if speaking in a code. She preferred the talk of intellectual people and didn't let men consider her a woman of kitchen and bed.

These men! she told herself, how happy they are with their own talking. So you have a simple, or difficult, general, or even common, definition of happiness. What then? You can't change anything with talk. Manijeh preferred to sing, rather than have stupid discussions with men who just boasted for each other. A song by Marzieh was singing in her head. The moon watched them in silence. Manijeh imagined the moon had a sneer on her shiny round face, as if to make fun of their discussion. Happiness!

"Well, Mr. Hamed," said Bahman, "give us your simple definition of happiness in one sentence, not more."

"Yes, one sentence," Hamed said, "just one sentence. Happiness means to be pleased with one's own self."

The silence lasted only a few seconds. A piece of wood in the fire burst with a loud noise, and Abdolah's hysterical laughter burst in the silence of the forest, lake, moonlight, and tents, in the hidden animals and the birds in dreamless sleep. They all looked at Abdolah, astounded. Nobody had said anything to laugh at. They waited for Abdolah to explain his laughter, but he became quiet. He stared at the flames spreading heat and light, without caring about silence or laughter.

Ready to defend his idea, Hamed sneered at Abdolah and said, "Which part of my definition was funny?"

Abdolah turned from the fire to Hamed, surprised. "Me? I didn't mean it. I didn't laugh at your idea. Tell the truth, I didn't hear what you said. I laughed at Bahman's question. Happiness!" And Abdolah burst into laughter loudly again. The others laughed with him involuntarily, except Hamed, who was like a fighting cock ready to defend himself. Homa put her hand on his knees and pressed. Like a very loyal dog she had something to say, but she was unable to utter it. She wanted to say, "Don't worry my dear, people are jealous." That sentence she had repeated many times in the past twelve years of their common lives. The only sentence she imagined would comfort Hamed in these situations.

"Is it possible to explain your idea?" Bahman said. "To be pleased with one's own self, how is that attained?"

Abdolah hid his laughter, pretended to be serious, like a student in the classroom and said, "Can I explain it?"

Bahman glanced at Abdolah, then at Hamed and said, "If Hamed agrees, you can."

Manijeh still sang Marzieh's song in her head, enthralled with the beauty of night, with the heat of the fire and the breeze coming from the lake. She seemed to wake from a dream, abandoning the song in the middle, and with the indignation always present when she addressed Abdolah said, "Why are you going to explain Hamed's answer? Hamed has a tongue and knowledge of everything and is qualified to speak about happiness. Did you forget that you always deny happiness?"

Abdolah felt betrayed, as he always did facing his wife. If his wife permitted, he could explain Hamed's comprehensive definition of happiness. "To be pleased with one's own self." When and how was someone pleased with his or her own self? Anyone who hadn't even one star in a sky full of stars might be pleased with their own self. The hysterical laughter rushed to Abdolah again but he controlled himself, and stared at his wife.

Manijeh was ready to answer Bahman's question. She was studying sociology at university and knew by heart many ideas from ancient and contemporary philosophers, from post-modernism and post-structuralism. When she had a chance, she sometimes talked about them to friends or to Abdolah. She had a big mouth, and was proud of her ideas. Manijeh had read a lot of definitions about many processes of life, difficult or simple. She could give a solution to many problems, but she was bewildered. Why couldn't Abdolah, with his Master's in accounting, successfully find a job, although it was said that his qualifications were in high demand in Canadian society? He hadn't been able to find a job in his field. He had experience delivering pizza, driving a taxi, as a courier, running a discount store, but these kinds of experience weren't worth a cent in Manijeh's view. He was a bread-eater instead of being a breadwinner. Manijeh, who worked and studied in university, who commented on the opinions of many classic and modern sociologists, wasn't able to force Abdolah to have the discipline necessary to succeed. She was disappointed in him and didn't respect his opinions. Even though he always worked, his work was like a seasonal resort, from one job to another. His income did not count either.

Hamed finished his comment, but neither Abdolah nor Manijeh listened to him. They were busy with their own definitions and personal problems. Bahman and Homa, who were listening, didn't understand much. Homa didn't trouble herself to listen closely. She agreed without listening to him. She had learned him during their common lives, and would swear by him and his knowledge. Happiness was evident in her pleased look, her sleepy talk, her languishing behavior. To be Hamed's wife was the symbol of a perfect happiness.

While Hamed was talking, Manijeh arranged sentences in her mind. She wanted to explain, to include many philosophers and make her idea strong and effective. She said, "I believe happiness is obtained by hard work and discipline. In my opinion, happiness doesn't descend from the sky for anybody. One has to try hard and have discipline in work. For example, the solar system, the four seasons, the fall and spring, the plants and trees. There's no fault in nature." She reasoned so much that everyone ran out of patience.

Abdolah said, "If the bald man was a doctor, he would cure himself. Give an example of your own happiness."

But as Manijeh started to describe her own happiness, Abdolah raised his hand to say, "It's enough." It was his turn to give his idea, which was that, in his opinion, happiness didn't exist in reality, but could exist in a dream.

This time Hamed laughed loudly. Abdolah said angrily, "Why are you laughing?"

"For the same reason that you laughed at me," Hamed said.

To stop the argument between Hamed and Abdolah, Bahman asked Abdolah, "Have you an explanation of your idea?"

"For sure I have," Abdolah said, "I believe in Omar Khayam's philosophy." And he cleaned his throat and read in a louder voice.

"Come friend, let us lose tomorrow's grief
And seize the moments of life:
Tomorrow, this ancient inn abandoned,
We shall be equal with those born seven thousand years ago!"

Without giving the others a chance to say anything he continued,

"How long shall I grieve for what I have or have not
Over whether to pass my life in pleasure?
Fill the wine-bowl — it is not certain
That I shall breathe out again the breath I now draw."

Abdolah's poetry was interrupted by the sound of clapping and praise, which meant it was enough.

"I wish we had read poetry instead of talking about happiness," Bahman said.

"You made the fire, you should extinguish it, too," Manijeh said. "It's better to sing."

Manijeh was more interested in singing Marzieh's song, but Hamed said, "Let the two others give their own ideas and have a conclusion, then . . . "

Manijeh was annoyed. "Then it will be time to go to bed," she said, "happy people are supposed to sleep on time."

Hamed was insulted by Manijeh's remark, but chose to say nothing. The woman and her husband had some stinging words for him, he thought. Perhaps his wife was right, people were jealous of him. Anyhow, they had come camping to enjoy themselves.

"Homa should give her idea," Bahman said, "I'd like to be last."

"I don't have an idea," Homa said, "my idea is the same as Hamed's"

Everybody protested. "Homa should give her own idea, too," Hamed said.

Homa said, "In my opinion, happiness is what you explained."

"What about yourself," Manijeh said, "what is your own definition of happiness?"

Homa pondered for a while – herself? Herself? And said nothing.

Bahman said, "We're waiting."

"I'm happy," Homa said, "that's it."

Then it was Bahman's turn. Bahman began with the others' definitions. Then he read, "*Happiness is running after wishes, not to reach the wishes.*"

All of them protested.

Abdolah said, "Repeating sayings isn't a big deal. Give us your own idea."

"I don't have a clear idea yet," Bahman said, "I'm studying and researching it. I'm asking people so I can find a comprehensive definition of happiness."

Manijeh couldn't stand it any longer. The song was flowing in her like a river. She let her voice echo in the silence of the lake. She sang a few songs from Marzieh, Elaheh and Homeira. All of them were enthralled by her song and her loud, clear voice breaking the dark silence. Everybody meditated on her songs, like a balm after the stinging words about definitions. When the fire died, the moon disappeared behind the forest trees, and the lake fell asleep in darkness, Manijeh stopped singing.

The group went back to their own tents. All of them were awake late into the night, thinking about happiness. Hamed was doubtful about what he had said. For the first time he felt he was not happy with his wife. To him, she seemed stupid, and her stupidity was clear to everybody. He thought about twelve years of life with her, the many times she behaved like an illiterate person, blank to every aspect of life. Like a dog who knew what to do to please him. He envied Abdolah living with Manijeh, a woman full of knowledge, a spiritual intellectual. A woman with independent ideas and opinions. A woman complete by herself.

Homa lay down in her sleeping bag, listening to the silence, and found she didn't like her husband as she did yesterday or during the past twelve years. The man was too proud of himself. He didn't consider anyone else, especially her. Only himself. She reviewed her past with Hamed, and remembered how many times she had been ignored by him, regarded as no more than a housekeeper, never asked her idea about a single thing. When she fell asleep, a trace of tear wet her face.

Abdolah regretted his own hysterical laughter. He shouldn't have hurt Hamed. He believed Hamed was a good-hearted man and deserved to be a happy man, even though his wife was so simple, she sometimes appeared stupid. But his own wife was a woman with authority and bossy manner. He glanced at Manijeh, who seemed to be sleeping, though in fact she was wondering as well. He saw a woman with admirable capabilities. Her voice, in the night's silence, had thrilled him. Her idea of happiness was thoughtful too. She seemed exceptional, and he wondered why he couldn't get along with her, even though she was always helpful and full of ideas about life, even aspects of life that he didn't care about. He felt happy in some ways, and was sorry that he had always blamed and denied her.

Manijeh pondered her own remarks. She realized she hadn't said all the truth. She reviewed her judgment about her husband. The man wasn't so easy-going and worthless. During almost nine years living with him, he had done his best. If life in exile didn't work for him, it wasn't always his fault. She accepted that a situation can affect a person's life, and for Abdolah the situation was usually against him. He had done his best, but . . . Manijeh promised herself she would be more supportive of her husband, less critical.

Bahman added a few definitions to his notes about happiness. Alone in his tent, he opened his notebook and in the glow of a flashlight he wrote. His plan was to create an encyclopedia out of the knowledge of people around him. In his opinion, ordinary people might have ideas more interesting than the knowledge collected in books. He was enthusiastically spending time and patience on this job. He could see a hundred or two hundred years into the future, when his encyclopedia would exist in libraries and be passed hand to hand. When sleep made his eyes heavy, he turned the flashlight off, put the notebook under his pillow, reviewed again the discussion in his head, and felt something stinging his flesh. What did happiness really mean? Did he have the right to pose such a question? Who was he, who gave him authority, to question his friends? Not only his question and his encyclopedia of knowledge seem ridiculous, his existence seemed like a joke. As sleep took him away he thought, "Happiness is an illusion, I will tell them tomorrow."

With material from The Ruba'iyat of Omar Khayam, *translated by Peter Avery and John Heath-Stubbs.*

Lelsey Anne Cowan

Rites of Passage

Rachel stares at her mother's breast, draped over the back of the chair in the master bedroom. A prosthesis slipped into a pocket in the right cup of a special bra. It is meant to replace, to fill up the contour of a whole woman's body; a woman complete with fertile curves and slopes and rolling fields of harvest. Like chest armour, it shields, protecting the imperfect image of femaleness underneath. Rachel wonders if there are any women who, like virile men in roadside diners, flaunt their scars, proud of their survival and strength. Women who consider the loss not an impediment but a liberation, like Amazon warriors who removed their right breasts to improve their aim with a bow.

Rachel tiptoes across the room, picks up the bra and holds her mother's womanhood in her hands. She carefully focuses on the sound of water splashing against her mother's naked body, behind the closed bathroom door just a few feet away. Her mother will not show her the scar, but Rachel has seen photos in medical textbooks she borrowed from the university library. Still, the idea is foreign to her, and like a child who draws oceans the size of puddles, there are concepts her mind just can't seem to fathom. The bodies in textbook photos are almost always headless, non-entities of science, things her cognitive mind can explain. But when she imagines her mother's face, green eyes, thin lips, brown hair attached to the framed torsos things cloud. She pictures her mother's chest, sunken, like a freshly-filled grave. Imagines the newly-amputated flesh she once fed off as an infant, on a cold metal surgery table. Whole, like an island surfacing silver water.

The shower stops. Rachel can hear the glass door open and shut. She gently drapes the bra back over the chair and sneaks away, through the hallway and living room, into the kitchen. The house is quiet, almost unlived in. Things are clean and orderly. Not like the scattered chaos she and her brother created when they were young. She feels like a tourist visiting the still rooms of a historic home. Although the doorways aren't roped off, she walks the perimeters, as if she might break something, or move it out of place.

It has been months since Rachel was home. When her mother was first diagnosed with breast cancer, over a year ago, Rachel decided to postpone her degree, but her mother insisted that she stay in Ottawa to finish. Rachel came back for the operation, but later visits were few, and never lasted too long. Her mother would have some reason why the time wasn't right, "too busy, too close to Christmas, too tired for guests." She downplayed cancer, the way she'd downplay a cold. Growing up, Rachel can't recall her mother ever being sick; or if she was, it was behind corners or during school hours.

Rachel was summoned for this visit home. Her parents put the house up for sale and her presence was required to go through the basement, see what she may want to keep before they "get a bulldozer and throw everything out."

"Sell the house? What's the rush?" Rachel asked over the phone. "Dad has one more year before retiring."

"It's a good time to sell. Besides, what are we going to do with all this space?"

Rachel guesses this announcement has something to do with her younger brother's pending return from Europe. She can't blame her parents for removing any temptation of offspring basement-dwelling.

In the kitchen, Rachel fixes herself a bowl of RAISIN BRAN with skim milk, the only snack choice available. Her parents have become health conscious as they approach retirement. No more OREOS, CAPTAIN CRUNCH or TWINKIES. The kitchen has been freshly-painted, strips of masking-tape line the edges of the cabinets. Fixing up the house to sell, like dusting the house before the cleaning lady comes. Rachel thinks of spiders, dutifully making a web, despite high winds. Like all houses recently sold in this neighbourhood, the bungalow will probably be torn down and replaced with a large generic house that is assembled with the efficiency and creativity of an IKEA desk. The idea of her childhood home flattened into layers of rubble is disconcerting, but Rachel prefers it to the alternative. She can't stomach the thought of another family living in her home, re-designing memories, painting over the walls that whisper conversations of her family's history. Even though her best memories don't necessarily come from the house itself, it somehow represents unity, the parentheses that hold together everything she has ever experienced.

New owners would reconstruct the aging house, mistake well-worn blemishes for deterioration, the way people see wrinkles as penalities of time, not rewards. They would compile a "fix-it" list: clean carpet stain; paint over pencil-mark slashes on closet door frames; sand-down the dog scratches on back door. They would wipe Rachel's existence clean within a week.

Rachel's mom comes into the kitchen in her bathrobe, a towel wrapped around her head in a terry-cloth turban. "Do you need any boxes? Because Dad has some. They're out in the garage."

"It's ok, I'll just use garbage bags. Thanks," Rachel replies.

"Are you in for supper tonight?" She opens the fridge and begins looking through the modestly stocked shelves.

"Yep. I think this is gonna take me a while."

"Good, we'll order pizza," her mom smiles and then takes her orange juice back upstairs.

These are the typical conversations Rachel has with her mother: daily transactions that avoid emotion. That way, the role of mother and daughter, care-giver and caretaker, can never be confused. It is not polite or uncaring, just safe. But it always makes Rachel feel unfinished, as if she stopped mid-sentence. Rachel and her mom never cross any lines; the space between boundaries is too vast and dry to traverse. They talk about dating, but not about sex. They talk about selling the house, but not about the reason why her mother has stopped sleeping in the same bed as her father.

When she was younger, Rachel never questioned their chiselled roles. Her mother was her mother, not her friend, as so many other moms claimed to be. Women who sat on the edge of the bed, wore jeans and gossiped with their teenage girls. And for that, Rachel has always been grateful. She had enough friends; she only had one mother. Now Rachel is older, and ready to be friends with her mom. She wants to know who she is, as a woman.

It worries Rachel that their relationship hasn't really changed in the past twenty-five years. Her superficial attempts at bending roles have failed, as if the umbilical cord that served as a safe and objective place of exchange between her and her mom still exists. It nurtures, but at a distance. Separate. If something were to go wrong, if a direct exchange did take place, the mother would recognize the fetus as a foreign object and reject it. Is this what Rachel fears? Rejection?

She hears the back door creak open and shut and sees her mom appear in the yard, dressed in her dad's old jeans, a frayed checkered shirt and work gloves. She grabs the rake that is leaning up against the tree, and tenaciously tackles the season. Her arms extend and pull, brisk and strong. The backyard is impeccable; she has spent more time there than in the house. For thirty years her mother has never hired anyone to cut the lawn or trim the hedges. At least most of the yard will be untouched by the developers. Perhaps her mother knew that all along.

The wind picks up and more leaves fall to the ground.

About half an hour later, she comes in, grabbing a KLEENEX off the counter, "Autumn chill's setting in."

"Would you like some coffee?" Rachel offers.

"That'd be nice."

Her mother sits down and Rachel pours.

Silence.

"How are you feeling mom?"

"Oh fine. Fine. A little tired every now and then, but fine." She smiles, stirs her coffee. It is a familiar grin that Rachel has actually caught herself doing lately. A forced smile that doesn't want to burden. Polite, meaning nothing, revealing nothing. The smile seen on the faces of caregivers to the elderly and elementary school teachers.

"Good. That's good," Rachel says, accepting her mother's diversion. "I guess I'll get started." She pushes her chair back, places her empty bowl in the sink and heads downstairs.

The furnace room is cold and dry. A single bulb hangs from a wire. Scattered around the room, in random dumping order, are the archives of Rachel's childhood. The problem with having a large basement is that there is no need for restraint when it comes to storage. A garbage bag or box full of keepsakes from each year of her life is tucked in behind old suitcases and stuffed animals.

"Rachel the bag lady," her mother would say each year, usually during the last week of school. It was Rachel's tradition to carefully select invaluable items and obstinately stuff them in a box, knowing that one day each item might have a purpose.

Unable to decide whether to begin with the newest heap and work back towards childhood, or vice versa, Rachel ties her hair back and plunges into the pile in the far corner, closest to the furnace. Squatting on her knees, she sticks her hand into grade two: an old green plastic bag that rips apart as she lifts it, spilling out yellow spelling notebooks, foreign coins, crayons. She studies each object, each page, searching for early signs of personality, or voice, something that she could identify as distinctively Rachel.

Once finished elementary school, Rachel works her way through her early teenage years, mostly binders and notes, found in an old LIPTON'S SOUP box, mouldy and wet at the bottom. It's a slow process; her hands become grimy and dry from dust years old. She can feel gray film lining the inside of her nostrils. She remembers why she decided to major in anthropology instead of archeology: too much dirt.

How does time discriminate worth? Why does it coat some items with memory and allow them to ripen, yet leave others to rot? A photo, a swimsuit, a finger-painting, on-switches that start the sepia 8mm film in her mind. Memories she can run her fingers over. A marble, a doll's dress, a plastic purse − what made her save such insignificant items? What things has she put aside recently, that will be questioned years from now? The importance of the present, forgotten with the past. Rachel will be illiterate if she throws away the Braille of her childhood.

It's getting dark outside. Rachel has been in the basement almost the entire afternoon. She piles all her keepsakes into a doubled garbage bag and puts the rest into a huge garden bag that her hopeful mother had placed on the doorknob. The house has been quiet for a while now. Rachel heads upstairs to see about ordering the pizza. When she turns the corner to the kitchen, she sees her mother's back at the kitchen table. The room is dim, only the natural light of dusk shading the room.

"Mom? It's so dark in here," Rachel turns on the light above the counter, illuminating her mother's pale face. She should have left it off. "Are you OK?"

"I'm fine," she says with the strength that protects a child from pain: an arm instinctively shooting out toward the passenger seat, when the car stops suddenly; the strong tongue clamping down on words that might elicit unnecessary worry. Rachel wonders if she will inherit this infallible nurturing, this self-sacrificing motherhood. Is it already within her, rooting and eventually surfacing, like varicose veins and early meno-pause? She sits down across the table.

"Mom, I know you're not fine. I can see how you look," she reaches out to hold her hand. It's soft and warm. She looks tired. Pale translucent powder coats the small wrinkles under her eyes, like a thin layer of dust.

"It's just that there's no order here. Boxes lying about. Old clothes piled up in the back stairwell. Even my kitchen's a mess. I don't have any control over anything anymore. Not even my own house." Her eyes rise to meet Rachel's. Rachel turns her head to look out the window.

"The house isn't so bad, only a few boxes. I can help you get every-thing together. It's not that bad," Rachel curses herself for her weak ef-fort, her generic response. She knows her mother isn't talking about the house.

"Oh, I know, thanks hon," she squeezes her hand. Rachel has failed her. Her heart races as her mind searches for a foreign language.

"You haven't lost control. God, you do more than most people I know. I worry about you Mom."

"I don't want you to worry about me," now agitated, her mother picks up her spoon and stirs her coffee.

"You're my mother, I am supposed to worry about you," Rachel says the phrase so familiar to her ears, yet foreign to tongue. The words her mother said to her as a teenager, when she left on dates with older boys who drove their father's cars. Don't worry, Rachel would say, standing in the front hall, her face dipped in blue mascara and bright pink lipstick, her torso squeezed into jeans so tight she had to use a coat hanger to zip them up. "But I'm your mother, I am supposed to worry about you."

Lying in her old bed feels familiar, but cramped. Her room hasn't changed since high school. She always considered herself a rather mature teenager, but the decor screams obnoxiously Young Miss and Teenbeat. There is still a collage of magazine pictures on her cupboard door. The clock radio beside her bed is on European time, so she could envision Stavros, her Greek backpacking fling, at the appropriate time of the day. To the right of the clock radio is a framed photo of her mother and grandmother, a stern woman, sharp bones protruding through saggy skin. A summer day, probably somewhere in Huntsville, there is a lake in the background. They are smiling, standing side-by-side, close, but not touch-ing. Their bodies are stiff, as if bracing against strong wind.

Unable to sleep, Rachel puts on her housecoat, and goes to the liv-ing room, where her mom is asleep on the pull-out couch. Rachel's heart-beat laps the faint steady breath of sleep. Quietly, she crawls up onto the bed, and lies on top of the thin wool blanket. The springs creak and she brings herself closer, curling her body up to her mom's stiffened spine.

"I can't sleep," she wispers, "Do you mind if I lie here a sec?"

"OK," she hears, from the darkness, and lays her head against the cool pillow.

———

"Drive carefully," her mother shouts when Rachel starts to pull out of the driveway the next morning. Her mother punctuates the end of all good-byes with cautionary phrases: "lock your doors, don't lose your keys, don't be long." Homonyms for "I love you."

Rachel drives through the aging suburban streets that she rode her bike down a million times, no hands, eyes closed. There have been so many changes in the neighbourhood. New kids, new houses, new stop signs along lengthy bends in the road. Official historic names are posted in parkettes, replacing the oral traditions of the suburban natives who named their sporadic green oases: the doggy park, rocketship park, the flower park.

Five minutes from the house, Rachel pulls up to the edge of the ravine where they used to walk the dog every Sunday. From the trunk she takes the garbage bag of keepsakes and an emergency winter shovel lodged below her suitcase. It has been years since she has been in this ravine, but despite the change in undergrowth, the dirt path remains almost the same. At a small clearing behind a chestnut tree, Rachel sets her bag down and begins to dig, quickly at first, then slowing at the hard underlayers of clay. She decides to dig wider, instead of deeper. Her arms and back ache by the time she reaches a depth that will suffice. Without resting, Rachel rolls the garbage bag into the hole and begins to cover it.

That night Rachel thinks of her childhood relics lying deep in the soil; corpses in a plastic coffin. She pictures phantasmic smokey strands of memories arising from plastic and paper shells and filtering through the air, like spirits disengaging from their mortal cavities. These wisp-like images float into her room, above her bed and hover over her skin, like fuzzy mirages on the peaks of hot rolling country roads. She lets the memories graze there, nuzzling at her pores and occasionally sneaking into her dreams in their fragmented, surrealist form. There, in her mind, she lets them flitter and frolic about in the waves of nostalgia, watching them carefully, as a mother watches her child, lifting heads above the water; protecting them from the strong undercurrent that attempts to pull them under.

Monica Noy

Mother Instinct

Did you ever think about us?

when he entered from behind and you screamed

and we screamed for you

mum

calling your name

Was he worth our hate our love our tears

mother

You were not perfect

You were not

m o t h e r

Was he so good you could leave us dump us?

when he fucked you

you fucked us

over

Why did you labour?

screaming as we entered the world

SCREAMING

tantrums at you in the night, giggling when you tickled us, spitting food on you, fighting each other for your love, dancing to your laughter, running from your hand, grovelling at your feet, singing for your amusement ...

MOTHERS ARE SUPPOSED TO STAY

not hurry their children to school then disappear

no goodbye

evening dew in morning sun

YOU were supposed to stay

Not ditch us

We were
children
you were
all
we knew

For a man
who   discarded
his
daughters
two
just like you

curlers deformed your head
in a rush
to remove them
you pushed us out
slammed the door
no goodbye

guilt
shared
even
cancelled
out

COME

let you come back

BACK

see the DAMAGE

Claim your right to be

MOTHER

SCREAMING   WOODEN SPOONS
SLAPPING   FLESH
HITTING
KNUCKLES

lavender scents sweeping dishes
soapy water baking cookies singing
lullabies hot chocolate braids and
kisses bandaids aprons tucking us
into bed time stories parks made
lunches   dolls   clothes   lollies
soothing voices open hands and.....

BRUISING
HOT CHEEKS

RED
BAWLING

EYES
THREATENING
SMACKING

TEARS
THROATS

PLEADING
EARS STINGING   OPEN HANDS AND....

YOU NEVER SAID YOU WERE SORRY

Joanne Vannicola

No Mercy

Despair metastasized in her bones. Mara thought there was no cure. She didn't know it was possible to become untied, to separate. She thought her mother would own her forever, claiming Mara as part of her flesh, like a mistakenly amputated limb. For Mara's mother wasn't whole without Mara, and wouldn't allow her to have a body of her own.

Hiding – inside or outside her body – was a tool Mara used whenever possible. If she could physically find a place to hide where she wouldn't be found, in closets, under beds, in cupboards, then she would. But, ultimately, not even a neighbourhood was big enough to offer a hiding place.

No one stops a mother from hurting her child. Mothers aren't violent. Mothers are nurturers, maternal, with only love in their hearts for their children. Mothers don't insist on bathing their girls at the age of ten. Mothers don't sleep with their children when they are lonely. Mothers don't touch children sexually. If a mother does, "she must have been crazy. It must be so rare."

Children have no voice. Children lie. Mothers love. Kids are bad. Girls are shameful. No one would believe the child.

Never, ever, talk.

Mara's mother knew she would never be caught. It didn't matter what was said or done. Mother is always right.

On the outside everything looked normal.

What does normal look like?

Smiling child. Mother hugs, puts her girls into music class. The mother looks like – normal.

"I sacrificed my life for you."

Mara never asked her to.

The fallen dreams of mothers - entrapment by marriage, the monotony of cleaning and cooking, the pain of birthing. Mara was at her mercy.

Mercy. Mara remembers lying on the bed, her mother's large frame hovering above. Mara looks over to the door. Above the door, Jesus is hanging on the cross. Mara knows they are being watched. Mara knows she is shameful, knows this happens because of evil inside her. Brainwashed to believe this. She can't stop her mother, can't be a good girl who won't be punished in hell, because her mommy is touching her.

Mother takes Mara's innocence away in her hands. Steals Mara's dignity. Her eyes look at Mara as if Mara is hollow. There is victory, gratification, in her mother's stare, as she carries out this act of infiltration. Takes revenge. There are secrets tucked between folds and crevices, suffocating in the smell of unbathed adult skin. Her mother finds pleasure in torture. Makes no sound, only silence. The screaming is in Mara's head. She cannot fight. Cannot open her mouth, cry or shout. Mara wanders, lost in the patterns on the walls, the thoughts of hell, of being watched. A tree outside the window, beams of sunlight form bars across the bedroom wall. Mara climbs the tree, enters the frame of a plastic doll, leaves pieces of herself everywhere. Perhaps, like Hansel following the trail of bread home from the forest, Mara might find her way back to her body.

Mara walking the shores of sanity, diving to the bottom of memory, salvaging pieces of herself. Mara reconstructing a self she could love, destroying webs of shame and guilt. Mara learning that to breathe on her own would not stop the beating of her mother's heart.

Twenty years following the trail of bread, Mara finds her way back from the forest, finds her own home.

Mara's mother did have power, power by virtue of being a mother.

Noreen Shanahan

Walking Memories by the River

We dream for our children
resurrect the ugliest visions
a rock to dangle over sharp cutting waters
drag a body from the river, hotly awaken.

Once a small girl strolling
along the Humber with her grandfather
became tangled with death
a woman's body against muddy galoshes
look away, he ordered.

The child now a woman
frame thickened
by the monotony of waking hours
watches walking memories unfurl

Imagines such a death, such a life,
dreams to clear a passage
carves pathways to trod
grips the miraculous strength

In ten wee digits
life dangles at the fingertips
a child reaches, trusts this touch
blood brilliantly roars into the next day.

Rosamund Elwin

Red is a woman's colour

Gladys hoisted her skirt, gathered wind deep in her chest, put one thin leg in front of the other, squinted into the heat, pumped her arm, and leapt high into the air. Like a cat, she landed on her two feet. To show they weren't impressed, the girls playing high jump with her sucked their teeth, crossed their eyes, swivelled their necks. Usually a shy, humble girl, today Gladys felt playful and clownish. She couldn't resist strutting about like a peacock.

"Beat that!" she said with a snap of her fingers.

Beth sucked on her front teeth. "Stop your boasting, I am going to whop your behind." Other girls shouted and hooted their agreement as Beth took her place at the starting line.

Gladys lived in a tight, tall wiry body. She loved to jump and run. She played net ball, rounders and soccer, but her favourite sport was track and field. She dreamed of competing against girls older than herself one day.

A chant started as Beth prepared to scale the skipping rope, held higher than the top of her head. "Go Beth! Go Beth!" her friends sang. Beth took the jump with a fast run. Her feet caught in the rope. She'd lost to Gladys again.

Gladys loved going to school, all her friends went to the same school. She had no sisters or brothers, and her mother was strict and stern. She thought about her mother. Her mother fussed and scolded her often. "Sit properly," she'd say sternly, if Gladys sat with her legs slightly opened. "A lady sits with her legs crossed. What kind of woman do you want to be?" Mama would ask, then she'd lecture Gladys about behaving like a `proper' girl. From these `talkings to,' Gladys learned a `proper' girl never talks to boys on the street corner, and if a boy is interested in her, he must go to her mother and ask permission to see Gladys. And, of course, a `proper' girl always sits with her legs crossed, something Gladys found hard to do. What was the use of that, Gladys sighed. Mother was so old-fashioned. The game was over. Gladys bade her friends goodbye as she gathered her dusty books and trod off to her class.

The next day was hot and dusty. Sweat ran down the faces of the four girls as they ran, jumped, laughed and teased each other. The game of high jump was exciting. It was Gladys' turn again to jump the rope.

"Come on praying mantis!" Beth screamed. The girls laughed at the nickname."Let's see you jump this high."

"Piece of cake!" Gladys yelled back. Her large teeth flashed bright in the sunlight. Every time one of the girls cleared the jump, the skipping rope rose higher and higher above her head. It was Gladys' turn again. She leapt into the air and something hot came out of her body. Jesus, what is that coming down on me? she thought, then silently asked forgiveness for taking the Lord's name in vain, a `proper girl'.

Before filing into the classroom with the others, Gladys ran into the bathroom, closed the door to the stall and quickly pulled down her underwear. She stared at a brownish stain on the white cotton crotch. Her heart pounded with fright and excitement. "I think I'm menstruating," she whispered.

Returning to her desk she sat through Mr. Timothy's boring history lesson and wondered if she should share her secret with BoBeth, who was quiet and did not hang out with anyone in particular. BoBeth and Gladys lived within walking distance of each other. Gladys enjoyed the times she walked to school with BoBeth. She found her funny and talkative. Gladys fidgeted and asked to be excused to the bathroom. On her way to the bathroom she met Yvonne.

"Wait for me after school so we can walk home together," Yvonne said.

"Eh . . . I don't know if I can," Gladys mumbled, entering a stall. She really did not want Yvonne's company.

The stain in her underwear had grown bigger and redder. She stuffed her crotch with toilet paper, and worried it would fall out as she walked. At her desk, she glanced at the clock, wishing it was time to go home. The minute hand moved slower than slow. Tick, pause, tock; tick, pause, tock. Finally, it was three-thirty, school was out. Gladys gathered her books and rushed out of the classroom. She brushed past Bridgette, who was waiting for her.

"Excuse me, Miss La-la-land," Bridgette said mockingly. "What is the matter, girl?" she blocked Gladys' path. Gladys pushed past her.

"I don't feel well. I have to go." She walked away from Bridgette, who stared at her as if she was an alien. Gladys could hear Yvonne calling out to her.

"Wait up, Gladys!"

"I have to go, my mother wants me home early," Gladys lied and hurried away. She did not slow her pace till she was home.

Gladys lived in a small wooden house, separated inside by a wooden screen. On one side of the screen was the bedroom she and her mother shared. Gladys dreamed of having her own room one day. She wanted a room like the ones children had in the magazines her mother bought every week. Behind the screen, Gladys quickly dropped her underwear. The bloodied piece of toilet paper fell to the floor. After washing herself and putting on a pair of clean panties, Gladys thought about what she would tell her mother. Her mind flashed to Rita, who had gotten her period last year, at thirteen. Gladys had hoped she'd get her period at fifteen, when she was almost finished school. Rita had changed after getting her period. She no longer played jump rope and hide and seek. She didn't race barefoot with them. Rita's mother told her if she did her womb would drop. Every month Rita missed a day of school because her stomach hurt so badly. Rita told the other girls she hated the bitter-tasting herbs her mother made into tea to ease the pain.

When Rita started to menstruate the other girls opened the diction-ary and looked up the word "menses." Then, they looked up sex, love, and other `rude' words forbidden by their mothers. They giggled with embarassment and the feeling of being naughty. Helen read out the mean-ing of menses, "Blood and dead cell debris that is discharged from the uterus through the vagina by adult women at approximately monthly intervals between puberty and menopause."

"Ugh! Yuk!" they'd exclaimed and went on to look up menopause and vagina.

Then Helen wrote the word "menses" on Mr. Timothy's blackboard.

"Who is responsible for this?" Mr. Timothy stuttered angrily.

No one owned up.

"You! You! And you!" He singled out Helen, Gladys and Beth. "Leave for the office right now!" The other students giggled.

Gladys threw herself onto the hard double bed. "How am I going to tell Mama?" she wondered aloud. Gladys recalled when her breasts started to grow, shooting out like small ears of corn. Everyone in the yard made fun of her. They didn't mean any harm, but she'd been embarrassed and self-conscious, wishing she could stop them from growing, but they kept growing bigger, rounder and higher. Then, one day, Mama came from work very excited.

"I bought you something!" she teased. She held a small brown package above Gladys head. Gladys reached for it.

"What is it Mama?" Gladys laughed. She grabbed the package out of her mother's hand. Mama watched her tear it open. Gladys loved receiving small gifts from her mother, it made her feel really special. But, this time, her face clouded over as she took out a white brassiere.

"Oh," she said, voice full of disappointment.

"Don't you like it? It's your first one. My baby is growing into a woman." Mama laughed. "Soon you will be getting `your friend,' " she continued, winking at Gladys. Gladys did not smile. She knew her friend was not a person. All the women in the yard referred to menstruating `as seeing their friend.' Mother showed her how to wear her first bra, but Gladys had never liked it.

Gladys pulled up her panties and went into the kitchen to greet her mother. "Good afternoon, Mama."

"Why so glum?" Mama asked.

"Mama, I think I got `my friend' this afternoon," she answered.

"What friend?" Mama asked.

Gladys groaned silently. Why did she have to forget now? "I have blood in my panty, Mama."

"Oh!" Mama exclaimed. Her eyes widened with excitement. "You've become a woman today." She grinned. Gladys thought she looked soft and pretty. "Red is a woman's colour, you know." Gladys felt her cheeks burn. What was the big deal? Why was her mother acting so weird?

"Go and wash yourself, then go into the drawer where I keep my cloths and bring me one."

Gladys left to do what she was told, happy to wash again.

"Are you ready?" Mama asked, coming around the screen.

"Yes Mama, I'm ready," Gladys answered feeling very shy. She watched her mother fold the white diaper into a triangle, then bring the pointed ends together to meet the folded, then fold it in two, to form a long thick pad. Mother spoke as she folded the cloth.

"Every month you must must wash these diapers till all the stains are out. I'll show you how." Washing the diapers was something Gladys had seen her mother do several times. She did not want to do it.

"You are no longer a baby," Gladys heard her say.

No longer a baby! Gladys felt scared.

"Pass me two safety pins," Mama ordered. Gladys' stiff legs moved towards the chest of drawers where her mother kept a small rusting coffee can containing clothespins, hair pins, needles, buttons, fasteners, and thread. She took out two large safety pins and handed them to her mother.

"Pull down your panties and put this in, then pin the ends to the panty, one at the back and one at the front."

Gladys followed her mother's instructions. She felt like dying, having to dress herself in full view of her mother's watchful eyes. Her mother was looking at her cookie, which Gladys had hidden since she saw the first hair appear. As her mother watched, she kept up her lecture.

"Now remember, you can have babies," her mother warned. Gladys wanted to roll her eyes, but didn't dare. She knew how girls really got pregnant. Before leaving Gladys to prepare the evening meal, Mama looked at her for a long time. Gladys thought her mother looked afraid. But she shook her head as if to clear it, smiled at Gladys and went back to the kitchen.

Gladys followed her mother, walking with her legs slightly apart. She felt awkward and uncomfortable, the cloth between her legs heavy and bulky. She worried that the bulge showed. She passed her hand along the seat of her dress, smoothing it down, assuring herself nothing showed differently than before. She plunked herself down on a stool across from her mother. Mama did not have to worry anymore, she would be sitting with her legs closed from now on.

Gladys snuck behind the screen several times before dinner to check how she was bleeding. She could not believe she was menstruating and secretly wished it would stop. She hated this day more than any other day in her life. Why did she have to get her period at all? Why couldn't it wait till she was much older?

Her mother's voice interrupted her. "Gladys! Come, come have supper. It is special, just for you."

Mama had covered the small wooden table with her special table cloth. The one she saved for guests. She'd cooked Gladys a special meal of dumplings and fresh crabs in coconut milk with callaloo leaves, tender and creamy. In the middle of the table was a pitcher of red KOOL-AID. Gladys' mouth watered. The aroma of the hot meal filled her nostrils. Was she hungry. She hurriedly dug her spoon in.

"Heh! Wait a minute," Mama protested. "Let's drink a toast to my daughter, who is a woman today." She raised her glass of KOOL-AID. Gladys did the same. They drank and smiled at each other.

brenda brown

in excess of blue

"I place a delphinium, Blue, upon your grave"
Derek Jarman

if i had known the colour blue when you died
i would have gathered the electric blue delphiniums
that grow tall in my backyard
the kind i would never grow again
i would have tied each long stem securely
onto the back of your harley
roared with them into the morning
we lowered your body into the ground

if i had known the colour blue
i would have painted your helmet neon blue
scraped away the last of your blood
with my sapphire chipped nails
i would have worn velvet crushed with indigo
and those suede boots
that would wrap around your waist
a blue streak down the highway

dead darling, if i had known the colour blue
i would have spoken my last words to you
with turquoise petals falling from my lips
knowing the only way to speak of your death
was with the grace of wild blue

for Bunk Shennan

Sharon Rosenberg

Cutting Through

carving poetry
out of wood
where what is
is not
is absence
a hole
or the parting of lips
aching for the caress of my lover's tongue
to cut through the shadows of memory

Sharon Rosenberg

Inner Curve

folds wet
from the spread of desire
cleft in memory

close my eyes
and I find you there
leaning into the inner curve of an eyelid
waiting
to rub chamomile-scented palms
across skins raw with longing
seeping histories of loss

skin unwraps at your touch
remembering
eyes hands torsos
layered one over another
til he shadows you from my sight

my body breaks, and
time escapes the bounds of linearity
flesh slips down to bone
where exhaustion etches
blood dries on my lips by morning
nausea, puddled in the throat of my fear

I wake without you

Sharon Rosenberg

While Hope Leans

despair chews into my lungs
til breathing is remembering
and memory is
my father's strangle hold
my mother's insistent lies
twisting back muscles into a knot of anguish
so what rises in me
is bile so acrid it
blisters and cracks my lips as I spit
past onto present

cell by cell
I unwind the knots
til a bundle of despair lies at my feet
soaking in the mucus of history
slip my fingers deep
into the hole remaining
in its wake
tracing desire
on walls
of fear
while hope leans parchment thin
against the doorframe
beckoning to this body
forgotten by dreams

Leah Darke

Half Mast

You leave the blind at half mast
so moonlight can kiss us in the dark
Bodies entwined
we drift apart
toward dreams

I've got you

Words encircle
squeeze me tighter
You invoke a spell
anoint me with promise
resurrection you cannot afford

I am struck by my joy
smiling
you've got me
and I'm your little girl

this blue-eyed child
who adores you
so much easier to love
than the woman I am

Annie Coyle Martin

Jody

"I wish once, just once, my mother would come alone to see me," Jody said. The light was behind him, fading in the big window, his face was in a shadow that hid the expression in the huge, near-sighted eyes. "Is that too much to ask?"

I didn't answer, because I didn't know his mother, and, in any case, it was more a statement than a question. He would mention it most evenings though, sometime after dinner and before the time we would both fall asleep.

If, in preparing dinner, I came upon boxes from a pastry shop in the refrigerator, I'd know his mother had visited on the weekend. He'd say his mother was here with Lucy from her bridge club, or with her friend Margaret. I'd change the subject to some gossip from the mayor's office, where the mayor was travelling that week, to a conference or a fundraiser somewhere, and that was enough to get Jody telling me stories of when he was the mayor's assistant, the youngest of all the city hall staff, fresh out of university and student politics. Then, before he could again complain that his mother always brought a companion with her when she came to visit, I'd switch on the television and let my weight sink into the corner of the sofa.

We'd watch *Fashion Line*, a commentator in a minuscule skirt describing with consummate fluency ensembles worn by gaunt, pouty women slouching down a runway. Jody loved that show. Most of the time we would both fall asleep. Jody in his chair and I on the big sofa.

We were both tired that fall. Evenings closed in earlier and earlier, the sky showed dark blue in the window and shadows gathered in the corner of the room. The year running out. Jody's snoring would sometimes wake me and I'd start up with a jerk, my neck stiff and awkward. I'd sit a minute, staring across at him in the wheelchair, his chin dropped forward on his chest, his scalp red and flaky through the few remaining blond hairs. Then I'd bustle about washing the dishes and tidying up, and before we knew it the front door buzzer would sound and I'd press the security release to admit the nurse from the agency who helped him bathe and get ready for bed. He'd come in smelling of frost and the outdoors and Jody would brighten up for a new audience. I was released into the clean cold air. I'd stand on the steps of his apartment building for a minute, feeling the long breath of winter coming. Looking south along the avenue of maples, with the street lights shining on the last of the red leaves, I'd sometimes see the brightest of the heavenly bodies, opportunistic, inscrutable Venus hanging on the horizon.

One November evening two red spots of excitement flamed on Jody's cheeks. "The mayor came to see me at lunch time. Just himself. He wants me back to work by January. I know I'll be better then, and he promised to put a sofa in my old office so I can rest in the afternoons."

Jody's funeral was December 29. We left the city at nine a.m. on a clear winter day. The vapour from the downtown buildings, rising straight up like incense, was visible in the rearview mirror as we drove north. On Highway 70, a gusty wind started and we could see it toss gyres of snow high in the white fields. Further north, clouds of snow began to blow in front of the car from the roadside banks. I could not see the rest of our group, following in another car. The road was a terrifying expanse of swirling white. We were not sure they had made it until they pulled in beside us in the parking lot of the old-fashioned country funeral parlour.

Exhausted from the drive and blinded from coming suddenly into the bright light, we crowded into a single row of seats at the back of the chapel. The oak coffin was massive with shiny brass fittings, and Jody's city pastor stood beside it, waiting with folded hands for the family. They entered slowly, the father tall and stooped a little, his brother stout and hearty, a darker version of Jody. Between them, in a floor-length mink coat walked his mother. When they were seated, his brother came back and invited our group to the empty seats up front, behind the family. The tiers of massed poinsettia gave a bizarre air to the proceedings, as if this might somehow be a Christmas pageant. I sat directly behind his mother, watching her quiet manicured hands curled in the fur on her lap.

The pastor began in a high voice. "Where is God's mercy in the loss of such a young life? What can we learn from it?" she intoned, and the listeners settled a little in their seats. What had I learned, I asked myself, wishing the service were over.

I'd learned about the marvel of electronic mail, each Friday when Kevin would set the schedule of who would sit with Jody and on which evening, and by touching a key on his computer, poll all ten of us. And we could respond instantly, confirming the dates, the news travelling over miles of optic fibres to offices scattered across the city.

I learned that it takes a long time to die, even if life is short. I learned to guard my tongue, talking only about tomorrow or next week, never about next year. I learned how the dying terrify us with their awful knowledge of what the end is like. And how we shrink from that. But I never learned if Jody got his wish, that wish he expressed so often in anger, frustration, or sadness.

"I wish, just once, that my mother would come alone to see me, so that I can have her sit there and tell her, `Mother I'm gay, and I'm dying of AIDS, what about that mother?'"

I tried to figure out if he ever got his wish, if they had ever talked about it, by watching the softened contours of her impassive face, perfect skin and small round fashionable sunglasses that seemed to hide eyeless sockets. Suddenly, I saw her lift her head up to gaze around and heard her whisper to her husband, "Arthur, did the mayor come? Is he here?"

mariko tamaki

Assignment –
Write a Lesbian Sex Poem

Course: LEZ 266A - DYKE LIFE 101
Due: FEB. 2

Write a lesbian sex poem.

The poem can be about someone fictional or real, but must be sexy.

Your poem can be one of several different genres discussed in class.

You could write a POLITICALLY CORRECT lesbian sex poem:
Use lots of food metaphors (remember to take advantage of all five senses). Be careful to always ask permission before moving in on erotic areas, even if it's only metaphorically - *Judiciously, the lustful lesbian paused and received a nod of consent before lowering her lips to her partner's awaiting nipple.*

You could also write an S/M lesbian sex poem, but be careful to oil and treat your leathers after extensive use.
(S/M poems will receive extra marks if they are situated in exotic locations: a phone booth, a university bathroom stall, even a stable. Use your imagination.)

This assignment will require some research.

Have sex before you write this poem, as often as possible and with as many different women as possible. Keep a journal on your night table, under your bed, or in your knapsack, depending on the situation. Feel free to use the pick up line: *Would it be possible for us to have sex? I have to write a poem for my lesbian life class.*

This should work.

Do not submit a sexy poem about bad sex - all bad-sex sexy poems will receive a grade of D. A sex poem about bad sex is a bitter poem (please refer to course LEZ 246A - BITTER LESBIAN LIVES) and is not within the course requirements.

Hand in poems for marking by 2:00 pm to professor's office.

Happy hunting girls. Remember, the hotter the poem, the happier your professor, and the better your mark.

Leah Darke

Elise was finally asleep. Tanya gently untangled herself and moved silently through the grayness. Elbows resting on balcony railing, she lit a cigarette. God, it must be late. She looked out over the cemetery. Drawing smoke deep into her lungs, the events of the evening unfolded on silent air. The roses. The safe word. The sobbing. Tanya's instincts were usually barbed wire sharp. Was it the roses? Tanya shuddered. She could still feel Elise's shaking body. Was she losing her detachment? A bad sign.

Tanya ran a rough hand through her cropped hair, lingering on the raised flesh of her latest tattoo. Detachment. She smiled. The rune meant strength. She was thinking of Elise when she bowed beneath the needle. Elise's strength, and her power over Tanya.

A whisper passed through the gravestones rustling leaves and raising the hair on Tanya's arms. How many were like us? Like Elise? Tanya did not understand Elise's appetite for pain, but she respected it. Tanya lit the candles, drew the baths, brandished the whips. Looking into a woman's eyes, Tanya read her hungers, her fears; coming back to write stories on flesh. Flesh like Elise's, almost too fragile for their play. Yet the blackness of her eyes held limitless desire. Hardened steel, her will unbreakable. Until now.

Tanya leaned back into the wicker chair, placed her long legs up on the railing. Elise hadn't spoken. Clinging and rocking, she pressed her wet face against Tanya's chest until sleep stole her. Tanya had brought women through before, but whatever happened to Elise was buried deep.

Her jaw clenched. There are so many of us.

Pink was beginning to chase the cemetery silhouettes. Tanya butt out her cigarette and stretched. She would lie open-eyed, next to her lover, until Elise awoke.

Excerpt from a novel in progress.

S.P. Larade

Crushed Velvet

We blow in together from a cold street, crackling laughter and seeking the intimacy of a corner, but oddly choose the luscious centerpiece couch of deep velvet dust – a much more elegant-appearing haven, than actual site, for our quick drink. We ignore the adjacent armchairs poised for conversational rebuttal, the lumpy sofa which will fit just two angled bodies, casually inclined towards the centre, an isosceles triangle of limbs and shoulders. Eyes bursting out at each other.

This getting to know you is excruciating and delightful and needs to be toasted with a fine assortment of amber liquids, a dark sugary molasses froth as richly toned as the wainscoted ballroom. Thawing from the street atop a wood stove, you toast us cheerily. "Up your bum!" as if friends say this every day.

I fall over your words, each telling stories of life amid shared sips – try mine, no taste this – much to the delight of the hovering waiter, his attentions verging on flirtation. We're oblivious to every other activity in the room, speeding ahead with anecdotes, dreams, regrets, confessions - a heady, fast-paced combination of sensations as second drinks arrive. An oblique toss-out: "My friends ask me what I'm doing seeing you two nights in one week and I avow, `oh she's my new friend' but I wouldn't be honest if I didn't tell you that I also have a crush." And continue babbling so that you don't have to respond, and I don't have to repeat. But it is out there, dangling, buffeted in the increasingly congested pub. Why is beer so delicious, smoky pubs so stifling?

The only pause in conversation is a pee break or two, then an aghast glance at watches, fluttering motions to leave and a lingering, longing to stay in the moment. Excited talk about future plans, more things to do, assurance that the evening has been fun. You have walked me home, escorted me to the subway twice now. Sticks in my mind as a rather gallant gesture.

Rescue: "Well, you know that whole crush thing you mentioned earlier? It's quite mutual."

Crushed red faces duck underneath hair falling forward, hoods and scarves burning hot, advertising. No denying those feelings. Safety net bottoms out. I am plunging twenty thousand leagues under the sea, a foreign substance fills my lungs and I cannot speak. I want to question what I have heard, incredulously. How can I walk away from this moment? I put out my feelings to clear the air, to be honest with myself and with you. You've been very clear. Now we escape, each to the homes where we'll replay what was said, how and when, and mine forbidden and explicit meanings.

I'm crushed out on you, thinking it's deliriously impossible, never in my wildest dreams could I have imagined, honestly crushed hyperbole. When you call and leave a message the next day, I want to transcribe every nuance, so I won't lose the feeling of you being with me, so that I will come to believe it.

Someone has to say it first: What is it we want? How courageous is that act?

I didn't trust my ability to hold the glass of draught and speak simultaneously, struggling to appear casual, relaxed. Calm, cool, collected.

Don't trust my ability to find the route home without the assistance of a compass and a finely detailed map. Next time I hope to walk you home, linger outside a doorway and struggle to tear myself away. Now you know, in fact, that I will talk all night long.

Lisa Ayuso

Wife's Feminesto

It seems foreign to me to start sentences with me, mine, I, my name. These pronouns go near the end, behind you that starts the sentences. It's like this: you and then I. You and then four steps back, me. Secondary. Second prize, only and if the opportunity presents itself. When my (hidden) anger, when my foul mouth still tamed for your standards, my irrational temper, my inherent stubbornness, my . . . what did you call it, oh yes, my ugly side, when my ugly side comes forth spewing like venom, I suppose the opportunity does not present itself. Well, today opportunity found me.

Desire is sweet revenge.

Suddenly, I feel the need to justify what's left of me. To start and continue and end with me, mine, I, my name to claim identity, entity and ownership of thoughts, feelings, of love lost for the small neglected moments I never could enjoy. And I figured it out, figured you out. I realized that everything you hate is mine. Mine, Mine, Mine. I scream this with the will and lungs of a two-year-old child. This is the first word I own, the first word that gives me power. Mine.

I often wonder at what point in my life did you decide/did I forfeit/did we agree on you having full custody of my body, my soul, my mind. I watch how my life, like a share in your company, drops in value and substance. I watch the fall of memories and all that you hold tight in your hand. Gone. But yours is not where I am going with this, it's mine, remember? My desire to want and be on my terms - to think on my terms. Not your words, my dreams. Not your future, my now. It's amazing how desire sprouts chance. I never had chance like you do. I've pondered many nights if you could ever feel fear the way I do. The fear of change. Just when I thought I could never give you anything you already didn't have, I found change. And don't think that you can size me down 'cause that doesn't work anymore. You'll try, try again, this I know. Your determination truly inspires me, it really does.

This is what determination looks like in my words:

I have . . .
I want . . .
I am . . .
I will . . .
I take . . .

Sentences that start with me.

And just so you know, for your own records. Just so that you can compare and scrutinize and use as evidence back to back, here is what you have left and what I am building.

Left - you	I Building
Everything I gave you	Desire
Without a fight.	To take back,
	To want more,
This is not unconditional.	To keep what I need,
	To never give you what is
This is not forever.	Not yours.

I am at the beginning and end of this sentence. I can do that now. I am in this sentence confused as to where you'll go. Over and over, I question why you would ever believe that this and me and all the haves that are solely mine were ever for you in the first place, like you deserve anything more. For this reason alone, I don't know if there will ever be room for you in my sentences.

For now I will continue as follows: Me first.

Things I need to do today:
☐ Me
☐ Mine
☐ I
☐ My name

Include all the above in everything.

Zoe Whittall

Hands Out

"Of course I know nostalgia can't penetrate a real city."
Gail Scott

"We have coffee covered, baby-doll," her weathered hand stretched out, holding a new weapon in our two-woman battle against poverty. We had officially become neighbourhood prom queens. Her hand held a SECOND CUP *buy-5-get-one-free* hole puncher. Those perfect little coffee cup designs we'd been trying to emulate with pointed pins. Now we had luxury lattes whenever the urge occurred.

Today we hit the big time at twelve. We feverishly tried to maintain equilibrium and sense of self. Sense of self gets dizzy and shakes with raw sugar packages in our clenched palms.

"Ever notice you get inflated confidence with alcohol and panicked discontent with caffeine?"

"It's a fierce fuel," she mutters, swallowing a smile.

The SECOND CUP Granité made it's first appearance and St. Laurent was filled with motivation and the bustling bodies and gaping turned-up lips that read, "I made it to the thaw!" Spring brings dirt closer to our bodies and it's welcome. Layers of long johns peel off, my exposed skin shyly stings. The straws go into the plastic cups, the brave go without tights under obligatory dark-hued plateau dresses. The harmonica-busking lady plays with new breath on Prince Arthur and people Make Plans.

Iced coffee goes hand in hand with the new-you resolution revolution. It's the *should-I-stay-or-should-I-go* debate, spoken as if leaving Quebec was a new idea. It's always under the surface, easily read between the lines on our faces. The need to bolt somewhere where a foot could get caught in the door. Somewhere, perhaps, without such discernible seasons.

People who live here, people like Jess and I, are resilient. I realize this in our espresso fervour as I'm keeping half her body out of the dumpster behind the Portugese bakery on St. Dominique. Twelve loads of pumpernickel. No mould.

"Food from the Gods," Jess muffles from inside.

There is a lot that can grow here, with its excess of nothing. From a gleeful glance over a Granité we could do anything. The *should-I-stay* debate drools off the lips at every second table, when Jess and I are on latte #13.

Where does this loyalty to our front stoops come from? We hear the pot of gold is in Toronto. We all know someone who actually got a grant there, or at least a job without a hairnet or assembly line. Maybe tumultuous times breed passionate creations. Or maybe we're just reluctant to leave somewhere with such low expectations.

Jess looks up from the paper, "Did you know Montreal has the most strip clubs of anywhere in North America? One of the highest rates of youth unemployment and the highest rate of heroin usage?"

"More cases of HIV on the island than the entire continent of Europe," I add.

"Kinda neat."

My coffee-stealing, dumpster-dealing sidekick is actually from Toronto.

"It's like living in a bland, pseudo-American city. I have no ties to it, really. Toronto inspires the need to make money or maybe buy new platform boots. But write the great Canadian novel . . . not a chance."

Lucky we have no such lofty dreams.

My roommate wanders in, "Do you ladies ever see the land outside the Second Cup?"

We give him a latte.

"I saw Leonard Cohen at Quatre Sous this morning. He's really much shorter than you'd expect."

We go home and make cinnamon toast for hundreds. All reborn on the first day of sun. We plan a canoe trip. A bilingual performance cabaret. A juggling troop. A publishing house. Then a detailed plan on how to rob a Brinks truck.

Jess and I sit on the roof when the sun goes down, pens poised and ready to shoot straight across the pages of our journals.

We shake too much to write it all down. We put our hands out and compare vibrations before refilling our bottomless cup.

Kids these days, mutters an old guy we see everyday on the patio, *they just don't believe in angels.*

Lesley Anne Cowan

Hair

Claire retrieves David's hair from the bathtub drain. The strand is light, translucent, like fishing wire. It tenaciously clings to Claire's sponge, wagging its tail through AJAX blue suds. Its determination impresses her. She picks it up and places it on a piece of toilet paper. The hair sticks like a crippled insect on wet pavement. Snapping off her yellow rubber gloves, she walks to the bedroom and takes her photo album off the bookshelf. Squatting on the bathroom floor, between toilet and sink, she places the hair, still wrapped in wet toilet paper, at the back of the album. She will add it to David's designated page later.

Claire turns the pages of her collection. She has been gathering strands of hair from friends and family and pasting them in a photo album since she was twelve. No two are alike: some are fragile and brittle, some strong as a violin bow, some have bristled ends that split, some are darkness fading to white. She picks them off coats, scarves, hairbrushes, pillows that once cushioned lovers' heads. She is discreet, quickly slipping the disembodied strands into a small plastic zip-lock bag from a supply in the side pouch of her purse. Once home, she writes the person's name on a small piece of paper and places it at the bottom of the page. She then releases the fine strand and allows it to free-fall to its sticky grave where it will land in its natural position: curled, straight or bent. Extra points for artistic interpretation.

Claire hears the familiar sound of keys scratching in the lock down the hall. David. She knows this because after living with someone for over a year, seemingly generic movements become as distinctive as voice. David is a heavy, off-beat stride, a high school hockey injury that delays the right leg; he is the impatient slamming of doors without turning the knob; he is the morning tapping of razor against sink with the steady accompaniment of running water. This is co-habitation: the familiarity of a body moving through a house.

David's face appears in the bathroom doorway. An initial bewildered look is immediately replaced by a dull glare, an expression that demands less effort on tight skin no longer pliant enough for youth's creative pantomime. Although David is only twenty-eight, Claire notices that his face has settled into the fixed severity of forty.

"Hey Hon," he says casually. Claire knows she must look odd, wedged by the toilet, but his silence makes her feel childish, instead of potentially whimsical. It's his way of belittling her. Not acknowledging her idiosyncrasies. David is a strong believer in Pavlovian conditioning: ignore bad behaviour and praise good.

"Did you get the wine?" Claire asks.

"Yep," he crouches down to her, lifts her leg , rolls down her woollen sock and kisses her smooth ankle. His soft lips are warm.

"Another specimen?" He nods toward the album.

"No. Not today. Just reviewing." Claire says, rising. She has no interest in maintaining conversation. There is nothing left to talk about. "I'll start dinner." _____

The first time Claire showed David the album he stared at her as if she had just revealed she was released from a psychiatric ward. "Jesus Claire, you should have told me you were psychotic before you moved in with me. I would have padded the walls for you. Where's your box full of limbs from your favorite relatives?" He had an eerie way of disguising harsh opinion in the form of a dry joke, the kind of joke that chaffs, but doesn't break skin, because there is always the possibility you are reading too much into it.

Claire had no verbal ammunition for his playful challenge. Too much effort. The idea was too shapely for him, too bulbous to be hand-fed through his linear brain. She had been collecting hair for so long, it was as habitual as brushing teeth. The custom started on her twelfth birthday, the day her mother died. She can remember being cradled over her father's shoulder, that night, secure arms carrying her sleepy body up to bed. A single strand of her mother's long dark hair stretched across her father's shoulder, as if still attached to her mother's body. After her father turned out her light and shut the door half way, Claire took the strand pressed between her fingers, tenderly drew the length of it along her lips, and then placed it in the back page of her photo album.

Claire had never understood why it was considered normal to collect ticket stubs, wine corks and stones from sacred monuments, yet abnormal to collect hair. A photo is a mere image, faded and pressed between pages like a dried leaf. An entirely different entity, completely void of the life that once pulsed through its veins. All the photos of her mother would never compare to that piece of her encased in plastic like a preserved bug: something Claire could touch, smell, even run her tongue over.

Claire's apathetic silence lingered uncomfortably in the air. David pulled her to his lap, put his arms around her waist and gently swayed her like a child.

"Oh, come on Claire." David grabbed for the album. "I'm kidding. You have to admit it's a little odd. But that's why I like you. For the surprises. Everyone has their little idiosyncrasies."

His last girlfriend collected beer coasters.

―――――

Despite their differences, Claire needed David. He was her source, a well-spring from which she drew traits she knew she would never have. Clear-headed and rational, he engineered their relationship into mathematical ratios, him:her, sensible:impractical, domicile:feral. They balanced, stabilized, and then divided by a common denominator, love. Commonalities of life that used to pass by unknowingly became important to Claire. Watching TV, playing cards, even cooking dinner became exciting because David's presence lifted her spirit, but weighed down her nomadic nature so low, she thought she would grow roots right through the kitchen tile.

She met him at a bar when she was twenty-three. Claire had just come back from Spain, where she spent five months contemplating the fact that she had no idea what to do with her life. At first David seemed enigmatic, but after just a few dates, Claire realized her first impression was wrong. His offering was simple and real, held out flat on the palm of his hand. A directness Claire found even more enticing.

"You keep me . . . irregular," he said, making Claire think of PEPTO-BISMAL. Then, he took her hand across the restaurant table, "What I mean is, you bring out the spontaneity in me." Immersed in the corporate money world, David craved novelty. His greatest fear was that one day he would look in the mirror and see himself naked when he was really wearing a suit. "Corporate conformity will suck the personality right out of you, if you're not careful." David found no constants in Claire. Sometimes she liked meat, other times she was a vegetarian. Her hair colour changed weekly, influences dependent upon inexplicable random sightings, the shade of an autumn leaf or the hue of her next-door neighbour's golden retriever.

Three weeks after their meeting, she moved into his two-bedroom duplex. In the beginning, their relationship was mostly physical. They spent weekend mornings lounging in bed. David read the paper, Claire stretched out beside him, travelling his nakedness with her eyes. It was a limited way to experience a lover, but eyes were the only instruments with which she could explore him. They didn't share the spiritual passion of lovers whose bodies were mere instruments of a deeper love. Instead, Claire had to rely on her corporeal senses with David – touch, smell and taste. She could only travel along, not into or through. Her greatest fear was that one day she would reach the end of him and fall off.

Before going to sleep she would ask him to lie on top of her, his weight resting on his arms wrapped around her body. It was the only way she could truly rest. "Won't I smother you?" he asked at the beginning, levitating his body over her delicate frame.

"No, it makes me feel safe," she replied, pulling him back down onto her. She didn't tell him she needed the weight. That he kept her in place. As if a breeze might come through the window and scatter her.

———

David thinks he knows Claire, the way one knows his child or the habits of a pet cat. He can predict her moods, when she needs to be held and when she needs to be drawn a bath and left alone. But there are many things David doesn't know. He doesn't know that she doesn't believe in God, but prays every night anyway. He doesn't know that when she jolts awake in the darkness, sweaty and confused, she is dreaming of her mother. He doesn't know that at the back of Claire's album, beside his hair specimen now mummified in a stiffened KLEENEX mold, is an unidentified plastic bag containing the wispy blonde hairs of his Tuesday lover.

Claire found the first three long strands sprawled out on the duvet cover three months ago. They stretched and curved, flirtatious and glistening in the morning sun; their obnoxious pretense of entitlement threatening.

"You bastard," Claire said aloud and moved in for a closer look. She picked up the strands, trying to envision the body that so absent-mindedly deposited them on her bed. Was the lover someone Claire knew, or some cheap floozy from the bar that David visited every Tuesday for happy hour? Claire squeezed the three fine hairs between her fingers and watched them spring into their natural tight coils: a tall, airy, bouncy blonde, whose high-pitched giggle fueled lonely men's egos in dark, smokey bars. She ran her tongue along one of the flimsy strands and tasted hairspray, not the cheap aerosol brands bought at the drugstore, but a textured salon blend. Did she work with David? Claire savoured the flavour, ingesting their intimacy. Inhaling the scent that David felt when he breathed his lover in, nestling his nose in her hair on Claire's pillow.

Every Wednesday morning for the next three months, Claire found similar hairs lounging across her bed. It didn't take a genius to make the connection between her Tuesday night French classes and the foreign deposit on her bed the next morning.

The simplicity of the affair was embarrassing. Couldn't they have been more creative, met at strange hours in anonymous parts of town, using false names? Did it have to be so easy?

During the next few weeks, Claire looked for signs of guilt. Traces that could be followed by calculated conversation leading toward confession, but David remained constant in his affection and routine. She couldn't understand why he didn't just ask her to leave. What purpose was this woman serving? What purpose of Claire's was she taking away?

Even his affairs were reliable.

———

Peppers and onions sizzle in the frying pan, grease occasionally pinging Claire's skin, rudely awakening her senses. The rage Claire feels is dull. It doesn't pierce the lung or shorten breath. It doesn't clamp her insides. Instead, it swirls at the pit of her stomach, precise, contained, like a pinched funnel of water. She admires those crazed housewives who chase after their cheating husbands with bread knives or slash tires in office parking lots. She wishes she had their frenzied passion. Passion that is all consuming. Passion that she never felt with David, in love or hate.

The banality of Claire's thoughts does not surprise her. She is thinking about paying her Mastercard before tomorrow's due date, about cancelling her hair appointment, about calling her sister in Toronto and telling her to leave the key under the mat. Last minute details before she leaves. Claire doesn't question her aloofness, but instead allows her mind to escape to the shelter of the mundane, leaving her body to stay and react. It's easier that way. She realizes her teeth are clenched.

"Smells great, Hon," David's arms wrap Claire's waist, she feels his breath against her neck. He lays his head on her shoulder, "I'm exhausted. Too much overtime."

"Here," Claire pulls away and reaches for the bottle on the counter. "Have a glass of wine." She had bought two bottles of his favourite.

Dinner is quiet. The clanging of cutlery interrupts vacant conversation. David talks about his work. In response Claire smiles, nods, swallows. David doesn't seem to realize that Claire had stopped talking, really talking, weeks ago. After dinner, they retire to the living room and Claire opens the second bottle of wine.

"Any more wine and I'll be asleep," David says, sinking deeper into the couch and reaching for the remote control. Claire pours him a full glass.

Twenty minutes later David's glass tilts, the wine slowly trickles down the side of his hand and onto the leather couch. He is snoring with his left eye partially open. Claire takes off his shoes and wraps the crocheted blanket around his shoulders. Then, she walks to the washroom and reappears with a pair of scissors and his electric razor.

It's over too quickly. Somewhat disappointing; Claire would have liked to have drawn it out. She puts away the scissors and razor, takes a seat opposite David and studies his newly shaven head. There are patches of hair covering hard to reach dents in his skull, she leaves it for him to neaten later. The faint glow of the TV scatters soft light on his face. For a moment Claire finds humour in David's non-threatening state. His baldness makes her think of babies, or old men, ages when forgiveness is easily granted.

Before leaving, Claire gathers David's hair in a plastic bag and tucks it under his arms, folded across his chest. She opens her album and takes out both David's page and the plastic baggy stuffed with unnamed blonde hairs. She places them neatly, one on top of the other, on the coffee table in front of him. Then, she calls a cab, and carries her suitcase downstairs.

Kari Reynolds

A Caribouan Cruise – Misadventure Ensues

At the edge of Sheshatshui, my friend's village, Innu families were taking down a row of large canvas tents which lined the beach. It was the day after the Innu Eitun, a cultural festival which celebrates traditional Innu ways, similar to pow-wows in other First Nations. In the aftermath of the event Elizabeth, my friend, asked me to help pack up her tent, in which she had cooked and sold dishes of her tasty caribou stew and homemade donuts.

After all the rush and bustle of the festival, we were taking our time with the job at hand. We gradually loaded the tent, spruce tent poles, cooking utensils and an assortment of gear into the back of the waiting pick-up truck.

Suddenly a man called out something in Innu-aimun, and drove off. A flurry of excitement followed, and everyone leapt onto the stuff in the pick-up. I had no idea what was going on when I jumped in with them. I just knew that whatever it was, I wanted to be there. Francis sped the truck in his accustomed fashion, along the beach road and through the village. As we picked up more passengers along the way the story unfolded: a lone caribou had been spotted across the bay at Northwest Point, swimming toward the village.

It is not unheard of for caribou to travel alone. More odd was its presence so close to Sheshatshiu; a village full of hunters. By taking to the water it made itself especially vulnerable. If it's true that an animal will `offer itself' to the conscientious hunter, this one was not burdened by subtlety.

I thanked my good fortune that I had missed my ride home that day. Schedules falling into disarray is a frequent frustration and an occasional blessing in this part of the world. Allowing for what happens, rather than fretting over what doesn't, seems to be the essence of life here. Many times I have had to remind myself to sit still, eyes and ears open, and see how events transpire.

A spirited crowd gathered on the beach by the fishnets strung out on wooden frames, and watched as a boat went out to fetch the caribou. On its return the boat towed the carcass in the water. Kids waded out as far as the height of their boots allowed, hooting with pleasure. Some of them have never experienced the traditional life in the bush. It was a unique opportunity for kids and adults, hunters and office workers, to experience a hunt together. The fact that it was an easy kill didn't diminish its importance, as it brought the community together.

Two elders stepped forward to take care of the carcass. It is crucial to do a proper job, especially with caribou which are revered by Innu. There was to be no messing around, and everyone formed a circle around the elders to watch and learn.

The two old brothers, Pien and Mathieu Penashue, made quick work of their task, cutting deftly and with great care. I found it hard to see through the throng of people, and climbed onto a tree branch for an unobstructed view. By chance I had my camera with me, and took photos to record the faces of four generations of Innu as they focused their attention on the way things are done. When the task was finished, families took their share of meat and went home to cook their supper.

Later I sat with Elizabeth in her kitchen as she made a fresh pot of stew. Having seen the distribution of the meat, I asked who would be the lucky one to receive the magnificent antlers. She got up to make a phone call, then returned to tell me they were there for the taking and that I could have them! She called upon her husband Francis to get them for me.

When Francis returned he showed me what to do to clean and preserve the `rack' of antlers. With no similar previous experience, I watched with great interest, wanting to try my hand. I secretly worried that my obvious lack of knowledge about such things would cause Francis to say that I should leave it alone. Too often in my life men have said, "You don't know what you're doing, so just forget it." I was grateful that Francis had no such attitude.

To my surprise, the antlers were enveloped in a thick hide, much like what covered the rest of the body. With a strong, sharp knife Francis cut and pulled small pieces of hide from the bone. He explained that the flesh on the scalp, still attached to the skin and bone between the antlers, must also be removed. The process was bloody and painstaking. Rather than take up too much space in Elizabeth's kitchen, I took the messy business outdoors.

It took me the better part of a day to finish the job. Each antler had ten points, and the shape suggested hands curving out from the arm-like shafts. I decided to keep the hide that I peeled off, to preserve the shapely pieces. By taking the time to do my best, I became less clumsy and felt great satisfaction.

After washing everything off in the shower, I sought a place for the antlers to dry. A platform had been built in the trees behind the house for storing meat. I hauled the rack up and deposited it there, and draped the pieces of hide over some branches.

Before everything was dry, clouds moved in and threatened to rain. I chose a nearby sweat-tent as a refuge for my treasures. Just in time, before a downpour, I grabbed the goods and placed them inside. Several groundsheets were handy, and I threw them over the dome-shaped tent, weighing down the edges with logs. Everything was nice and snug, well-protected from the rain.

When the sky cleared I checked on my handiwork. Poking my head into the tent, the sight I beheld made me want to scream. Dogs had gotten in and chewed up the whole works! The delicate pieces of hide were gone, and the antlers had been reduced to ugly little gnawed-off stumps.

But my personal loss was the least of my concerns. One of the most important traditional laws of the Innu is to respect caribou bones. Letting dogs have the bones is a sacrilege. To dishonour the caribou was to offend the animal spirits, which could jeopardize the success of future hunts. I was in very big trouble. I concealed the evidence of my desecration in a garbage bag, and sat in the tent, smoking heavily. How would I make up for the damage I had caused? Would I ever be forgiven?

I was horrified by my foolishness, and gave some hard thought to how I would face up to my responsibility. My mind settled on making my confession to Pien, one of the elders who had handled the caribou on the beach. Preparing for the worst, I grimly packed my bags in case he told me to leave and never come back.

When I saw a chance to use a phone without being overheard, I called Pien's son, Greg. I said only that I needed to speak with his father, if I could prevail upon him to translate. I imagine that it seemed a strange request since I had never spoken with either of these men before, but Greg graciously agreed without asking any embarrassing questions. The only hitch was that he would be busy for a day or so. I resolved to wait in silent, lonely, and nervous anticipation until then.

That evening I was invited to a meeting of the Sheshatshiu Women's Group. Since only a small number showed up, the women talked casually without following an agenda. Anne, one of the younger women, provided translation in English. Discussion centred on the arrival of the caribou. Speculating on the meaning of this strange event, one woman suggested that the animal may have been a messenger. If it belonged to the George River herd it could have come south from Voisey's Bay. In that case, it was probably asking for help.

Voisey's Bay is part of an environmentally-sensitive region in the pristine northern reaches of Innu territory. It provides essential nesting grounds for endangered migratory birds such as the harlequin duck. Enormous herds of caribou depend on mosses in the adjacent tundra for food.

Recently, mining companies `discovered' the area, with its large deposits of nickel and other minerals. Now the area is threatened with a massive, open-pit mining development. Stakes were claimed, and `exploration' continues at a rate that would impress Christopher Columbus.

Translating for the older woman, Anne returned to the purpose of the caribou's arrival. Perhaps it came to warn of the danger to its herd if mining activity continues. (I tried not to squirm in my seat as I considered the potential importance of the animal I had unwittingly dishonoured.) It was significant that the caribou was alone. When addressing an elder about a problem, Anne explained, Innu protocol demands that the news be delivered by one person, or in this case one caribou, who is centrally involved in the situation.

I was stunned. This information was precisely what I needed to hear, relating two-fold to my own dilemma. It confirmed my instinct to go directly to Pien, without the benefit of asking Elizabeth to advocate for me. The knowledge that I was on the right track was a comforting gift.

I spent a few hours that night thinking about what I would say to Pien. There was much to explain. I wanted him to know that I am a supporter, not a journalist, despite the use of my camera as he and his brother dealt with the caribou on the beach. To help put my thoughts in order I wrote down everything I wanted to say. As a precaution against anyone getting a glimpse of my writing on the subject, I slipped the notes into my pocket.

A day and a half later, Greg drove by to take me to his father. As I put the offending article, still wrapped in a garbage bag, on the back seat of his car, I was grateful that, again, he didn't ask what my request was about.

Pien sat on the couch in Greg's living room. A toddler stood in a playpen nearby, and I noted with dismay that this meant I couldn't smoke. This wasn't going to be easy. After a minimum of pleasantries and small talk, it was time to cut to the chase. I opened my mouth to speak, but anxiety had me tongue-tied. Speechlessness is not a problem I normally experience, and it was particularly embarrassing at that moment, given that I had arranged for this meeting. A solution to my dumb-struck condition came to me: I still had the notes I'd made while sorting out my thoughts. I drew them from my pocket and, with a shaky hand, passed them to Greg for translation.

The first part of my message explained the small bundle of tobacco that I offered. I hadn't heard of this as part of Innu tradition, but among some First Nations people it is customary to give tobacco, particularly when requesting help from an elder. I handed over the bundle, wrapped in red cloth and tied with ribbon, with my left hand. This is how I was taught to show respect correctly.

As Greg translated my message, a smile gradually came to the men's faces. Several times they even chuckled. Under different circumstances I might have been curious enough to ask what was funny, but I was still too unsettled to share in the humour. Greg finished reading, and he and his father spoke solemnly in Innu-aimun.

They turned their faces toward me. Greg said this was the first time he'd encountered a white person who revealed and apologized for such a transgression.

My note included the theory I'd heard about the caribou at the Women's Group meeting. Pien had another interpretation; the animal may have come in response to the drum, which an elder used during the Innu Eitun the day before its arrival. The purpose of the drum is to call animals closer, to improve the prospects of an upcoming hunt.

So the caribou wasn't necessarily an important emissary for its herd. It may have been minding its own business, munching on some moss, until it was mesmerized by the call of the drummer. Perhaps I could take some small comfort from that.

Then Greg came to the main point. It is indeed a serious infraction of Innu law to give caribou bones to dogs. It is almost equally wrong to carelessly leave bones lying around. However, it was clear that I had simply made an honest mistake due to inexperience and naiveté. This is a different matter entirely. I felt my shoulders, which had been knotted up around my ears for two days, slip down toward their normal position.

We talked about religion, the damage caused by meddling missionaries, and the resultant loss of traditional ways. Greg circled back to the subject of my confession. He expressed appreciation for my respect for the caribou, the elder, and Innu spirituality. His father nodded.

Far from my being thrown to the dogs myself, I seemed to have gained some credibility out of the whole affair. In keeping with the ancient beliefs of my Norse ancestors, I thanked my Lucky Stars.

Pien stood up, pipe in hand, ready to go. At the door he turned, smiling, and with a wave made a parting comment. When Greg finished laughing, he translated, "If the animal spirits are pissed off, don't worry. We'll take care of them."

Leah Darke

N*ke

Ancient symbols
in a cheap velour bag
oracle invited by stones
made in China

Does carving the sacred
bring the price of rice?

In this world
seekers covet running shoes
Nike, goddess of victory
mass-stitched on the third world

1-976-DIAL-A-DATE

The LAST resort. It's my FIRST time CRUISING through the personals, decoding the HALF WORD GIBBERISH and LIES

SWM seeks 2BiF 4 HOT NITES

LOOKING FOR MR OR MS RIGHT (often referred to as Mr or Ms RIGHT NOW), skimming my finger along the newsprint as I listen to the mindless computer voice taunting . . .

TO MAKE YOUR SELECTION PLEASE PRESS ONE NOW FOLLOWED BY THE BOX NUMBER OF YOUR CHOICE . . .

Hurry up, the little voice inside me screams, this is costing you $1.99 a minute (8 minute minimum, I find out later), hurry up, your roommates are going to see the $20.00 charge on the phone bill and they're going to think you're having phone sex...

Aren't I?

BOX 57606
HI, MY NAME IS TODD AND I'M . . .

Can't fuck a Todd . . .NEXT

BOX 57707
YO! THIS IS JACK AND MY HOBBIES ARE CYCLING AND . . .

Can't fuck someone who says YO. That's disgusting. NEXT

BOX 50666
Hi, my name is Joseph and I'm 27 years old, 5'11, and I'm looking for

a woman 25+ who's in for some **DISCRETE SEXUAL ENCOUN-
TERS . . . did I mention I own a restaurant?**

HMMMMMM. DISCRETE SEXUAL ENCOUNTERS . . .
Cold fucking on a hard industrial kitchen floor. Imagine the size
of his fridge.
Maybe he'd cook something for me? Maybe something hot and spicy?

I leave a message.

Hi, my name is uh, ROSE and you can uh call me at 656-6495.
Maybe we can get together and make some . . . plans.

Click.

Am I supposed to get hot and heavy while leaving this message? I'm
flushed, already imagining Joseph (tall, dark and handsome) pinning me
up against one of those big restaurant grills, my fingers groping along the
ledge for balance, careful not to catch any knobs.

IF YOU WOULD LIKE TO HEAR YOUR MESSAGE AGAIN PRESS 1
TO RETURN TO THE MAIN MENU PRESS 2

To continue fantasizing and zone out this voice PRESS 3 NOW.

My message sent, I hang up the phone and slip under the covers.

DISCRETE SEXUAL ENCOUNTERS

fumbling for the lamp switch with my one free hand, those three
words, my phone sex mantra, lull me into a tender sleep.

DISCRETE SEXUAL ENCOUNTERS

The adventure has just begun.

sherree clark

garden

weeding

so here you come
trespassing on ground so old
it's probably gone to seed
I sit and watch with wary eyes
your arriving
and your being here
as if you were planning to entangle

and I know that you're not
yet I won't be sure until
I question all the plans
and rudimentary attempts
on your part to make
my garden emanate and
give way

roots

I'm undaunted as I try and convince you that I stand alone entwined in your limbs like creeping clematis. You smile and believe every word, leading my fingers over your flesh. And we listen together to my protestations of innocence, in this our growing, while intricate vines of blue-green foliage wind around our toes, bloom at our knees. And you say shhhhh, ever so softly to still the rustling of my heart. And you unfurl words of desire while I envision a forest deep and purple.

I am drowning in my own accusations of denial, you grab limbs which flail and writhe like a dreaming child. Bruises spread on your arms and legs like black water as you reach for me. And still I drown in fear, having seen your beauty. Eyes wide with terror and desire I am blinded by the gifts you offer, the bearing of them, now in me like ripe fruit, pungent and sweet.

pruning

Now is the time to whisper accolades of love. Time to take gently in your hands my face and say *you are all I want, need, desire.* Undone by your voice so close to my mouth I think, *yes, for now.* And you, not knowing that I choose to undermine, continue to speak of your love as if it were made up of tiny heartbeats pounding against flesh. As if it were small plumed birds caged and ready to be set free.

blooming

In this bed we planted the saplings that will withstand the drought and chill of winter. Tied gently to each other with bright red ribbon to ward off predators, the trees should grow separately as one. Spliced at the roots and cauterized, we nurture the rough beginning with fertilizer and some polluted water. If they are to grow healthy they must endure the true test of land rich with pain and stunted growths. Acclimatized, weathered, they should heave themselves through the dirt like submerged swimmers coming up for air. And then breathing and reeking of subterranean soils, they will radiate a fragrance powerful enough to draw birds and tiny winged creatures, who get drunk on white dust.

cornucopia

now that we've sowed a few seeds,
witnessed a nurtured growth;
fruits so ripe fell off
in our hands,
juices stained on our fingertips
and lips,
vegetables bulbous, green and red mutations
in a garden watered, pampered, eyed as
the seasons turn,
for signs of blight
spiders took up residence in the leaves
webs entwined around
stalks twice
to stave against strong winds
and fatted bugs blown
in on the odd storm

now that we've grown large
with the fruits of harvest,
run wild with our passion for sweets, become
tipsy on the nectar and fallen
at each other's feet with offerings,
loved with our bellies and mouths full
to bursting

now that we've gleaned,
shall we settle in for the long
dry winter, first
covering the soil
that now spent,
gave us this new light?

Noreen Shanahan

Her Breath on the Looking Glass

Undressing feeling
intellect a crippled thing
useless at disguises.

Roll back the sleeves to do battle
wicked slice through consciousness
she recoils – always these reminders of war.

Crash down drive deep
remove what bits remain alive.
A figure emerges softly drawn
her breath on the looking glass.

Calm eerily trembles
as flesh holds silently steady
a wave motions further into life.

The child races the wind
whirls past sharp danger
gathered into arms learning to love
despite weeping wounds.

Zoe Whittall

My Sister

I met her at the Michigan Women's Music festival a few years back. We stuck together 'cause she never used anyone's name, she just said my sister.

"Want some lentil stew?"

"Thank you, my sister," she'd say smiling, subtly mocking the land of separatist idealism.

We decided to stick together largely because we were confused. Like all couples who arrive at the festival together, my girlfriend and I were breaking up. She was busy sucking face with every surgical steel-laden lady on the land. In three days, I had seen only glimpses of her between the trees. Every cute girl I saw was a potential dramatic nightmare. Except for my sister. So we shacked up platonically in her tent and spent our time off unassumingly stalking Donna from Team Dresche, and sitting under trees watching the madness.

"I thought the festival was going to be chicks with hockey hair weaving rainbow baskets and singing KUMBAYA. But it's like two weeks at a lesbian bar." She summed our time up so accurately. Both of us just wanted to make friends, but no one was interested in a relationship that required little nudity.

Nothing was as much fun as watching San Francisco super-dykes wearing leather minis and $200 bras strut around.

"Do they not realize they're sleeping in mud?" my sister observed.

We rarely left worker camp except to sell our staff T-shirts to rich festie goers, who spend $300 to camp and eat tofu and watch Ferron with 9,000 other wimmin luvin' wimmin. It was cultural lesbianism at its highest and my sister and I reacted fearfully.

And, what I thought would end in a soggy POLAROID and an outdated address scrawled on a pack of cigarettes resulted in a long distance written affair and now, a cute two-room nest with a puppy and whole lotta stories.

Joanne Vannicola

Angel Eyes

The call came around nine p.m. Emily had been sniffing coke, beer chaser, with her sister, Jude. Jude was on the phone, Emily was jumping up and down to *Burning Down the House* by the Talking Heads.

Emily was seventeen. Jude hung up and started to cry. Emily turned off the music.

"What is it, Jude?"

"It's Tracy. Jimmy beat her up, kicked her in the stomach. She had the baby, and doesn't know if he's gonna live."

By morning, Emily was on the plane headed for Winnipeg, to be with Tracy and the baby.

What if the baby dies? What if she doesn't know how to deal with the situation? What if something happens to Tracy? Where was that fucker? Emily wanted to find Jimmy, get a weapon and hit him over and over again until he knew what it felt like to be in a lot of pain, to be afraid for his life.

Destination: St. Boniface Hospital. Emily walked the halls until she was able to calm her heart enough to ride up to the sixth floor, where her big sister lay staring at blank walls. Sad eyes. The sisters were ten years apart, completely different people. Tracy liked country music, guys, soap operas, and good old gossip. Emily liked rock, blues, women, and the big city. Winnipeg was too damn slow and way too cold.

They hugged each other hello without speaking. Tracy was in pain from the C-section, and sick. She had that same look she would get after their father beat her when she was a girl, wanting someone to make it all better, quiet fear and shame her shadows.

On the window sill was a plastic vase filled with silver cellophane balloons that said, "It's a boy." Emily wondered who the hell would be insensitive enough to send joyous balloons to a woman who was beaten until she gave birth to a premature baby weighing two pounds; tubes coming in and out of his little body, a baby who might not survive.

Tracy and Emily walked to the intensive care unit for the premies.

"I named him Sasha."

The sisters washed and put on their hospital gowns before they could get close to him.

Sasha was tiny, so fragile. It was hard to believe someone this little could be breathing. You could hold him in the palm of one hand.

Emily stayed at the Y across the street from the hospital. The room was a large closet, with a tiny sink beside the bed. Enough to hold a six-pack of beer. Emily had held her tears while at the hospital, trying to take care of her big sister, but when she lay alone, sorrow rushed from every pore. It felt good to release it. Three beers later, she relaxed into sleep.

Each new morning brought hope. Emily went to the hospital, spent some time with her sister, then with Sasha. More and more, Tracy kept her distance from the newborn. Some days she wouldn't even go see the child. The longer Tracy stayed away, the more time Emily spent with the baby. Some days she spent eight hours with Sasha, wishing for a miracle. On the phone, Judy told her that if she rubbed her hands together and held them above the baby's body, a healing energy would help him live. Emily tried everything, willing him to survive. The nurses taught her how to clean Sasha. When his tiny lips would get dry, she would moisten them with a Q-TIP. The end of the Q-TIP was bigger than Sasha's lips.

A test-tube was placed around his penis to do tests and catch his urine. He had another tube in his chest, and another in his abdomen. Finally he opened his eyes. They were beautiful. Blue grey eyes. His little spirit shone. An angel baby. Emily wound the musical bear, Sasha held onto her baby finger. It was wonderful to feel such a grip from someone so small.

In the evening, Emily would get take-out. Tracy had a big appetite, and hospital food just would not do. They never spoke about Sasha. Emily didn't ask why Tracy didn't see the baby more often. She knew Tracy was trying to protect herself from falling in love with her child.

Emily had always tried to help Tracy. She would sneak food to her when their parents wouldn't let Tracy eat; she would place her little body between her father's fists and her big sister's body. Tracy would never protect herself physically. She would freeze in place before the blows came, unable to run. Nowhere to hide but inside.

Two weeks passed. Sasha hadn't gained any weight. He wasn't urinating, and his colour was off. It was 50-50. Sasha could go either way. Something shifted in Emily. Rage started to surface, a rage that wouldn't calm. She had to find Jimmy. She had no idea what she was going to do once she found him. All that mattered was confronting him. She found out he was staying with his parents, left a message saying she was on her way to talk to him. It took her two hours to get to the house in the unfamiliar city. This man had chased her big sister with an axe, kicked her in the stomach during her sixth month of pregnancy. Somehow he was going to pay. Emily never thought for a moment that it could be dangerous. Rage alone, guided her.

When Emily arrived at the house, Jimmy's mother invited her in, offering tea. Jimmy wasn't home. He had taken off on the ski-doo. She wasn't sure when he would be back. Emily went in for a while, deciding to wait, and had that tea. They sat there staring at one another, talking about the weather, and Winnipeg, and every other annoying thing that had nothing to do with life or reality. Emily realized that Jimmy's mother knew nothing of the birth. After an hour, Emily left, unable to stand another minute of small talk.

What a coward, Emily thought, he could beat a pregnant woman, but ran away from her 17-year-old sister. "Asshole."

The third week of Sasha's life, Tracy was still sick and sore, still numb. Emily didn't mention her visit to Jimmy's house. Sasha was out of the incubator. He lay on top of a fluffy pillow where she could touch and see all of him. His skin was yellowing, his bright little eyes were becoming dull. His abdomen was bloating. New tubes entered his baby body to drain urine and bodily fluids. But it wasn't working, he wasn't getting stronger. Emily put her baby finger in Sasha's hand. No grip, though she could feel him trying to grab on, the pulse inside his hand.

Tears started to drip as she prayed for his survival.

Tracy joined Emily with the baby again. The doctors and nurses explained why his head was starting to bloat. Fluid in the brain, possibly blood. He may not survive.

Tracy and Emily went to have a smoke in the smoking room. Hospitals still had smoking rooms then. Tracy didn't talk about Sasha. She talked about other women in the hospital, about being hungry. She let out a big fart, then laughed hysterically.

"Farting's supposed to be good for ya. Anyway, it helps my gut. Would you go get some pizza, Em?"

Emily cried herself to sleep that night, wondering why Sasha wasn't improving when she did everything she could. Rubbed her hands above his body, sending energy, brought music, kept touching him, sending her love and hoping that it would be enough for him to live. Emily wanted to be held. This was a pain she had never felt.

The following day at the hospital, Emily couldn't believe how Sasha looked. He seemed bloated everywhere. His eyes were shut, she could no longer see their colour. There was no energy, no grabbing in his hand. His little fingers wouldn't curl around her baby finger anymore. The nurse said the doctor would be in to see them both in a few minutes. Emily went looking for Tracy. The sounds of other babies crying, and the smell of disease made her feel dizzy. Her heart was racing. Emily told Tracy that they needed to go see the doctor. Tracy had that frightened look in her eye.

Outside the intensive care unit they stood waiting for the doctor.

"He's not going to live through the next few days, we're sorry. You have an option. He can go on his own, which will take longer, or we can remove life support," the doctor said, staring in Tracy's eyes. Tracy looked at Emily, asking Emily to make the decision.

"Do you want us to help him go?" the doctor asked.

Emily nodded "yes," unable to speak the words.

Tracy immediately took off. Emily followed. Time for a cigarette. Tracy sat down and engaged in conversation with another woman in the hospital. Emily watched, smoked, and felt lost. She wanted to hold her sister, but Tracy wanted to run. Emily couldn't hear what they were talking about. She could only see her sister's face, talking and even laughing with this other woman. Everything slow motion. No sound. Just eyes, gestures, moving lips. Emily looked at the clock, back down the hall, at Tracy, and finally said, "I'm going to go back Trace. I'll come get you when it's time."

Tracy shook her head in acknowledgement, without breaking her conversation.

Emily ran down the hall to Sasha. There was a curtain drawn around him. Too late for one last touch. Emily stood frozen, tears just behind her eyes.

"I'm sorry Sasha," she whispered from the door.

The sounds of the machine could be heard. The monitor stopped. Emily ran, up and down the hallways, to the smoking room where Tracy sat, still talking. Looked into her sister's eyes, an up and down nod. Sasha was dead. Tracy lowered her head, allowed herself to cry. Emily went to her sister, stroking her arm, stopped her own eyes from leaking.

After some time, Emily and Tracy were brought into a small room, waiting for Sasha in silence, trapped in a small space filled with crosses and images of dead people. A nurse finally came in. Sasha was wrapped in a blanket and placed in Tracy's arms. She rocked back and forth with tears falling down her face. It was excruciatingly quiet.

"Do you want to hold him?"

"Yes," Emily whispered, her body shaking, not really wanting to hold a dead baby.

Sasha was passed to Emily as if he was still alive and fragile. Emily sat, pulled the blanket away from his face. For the first time she held Sasha in her arms. He looked less bloated, peaceful. Out of pain.

"Goodbye, Sasha."

It was late when Emily left the hospital. She didn't want to leave her sister, and she didn't want to be alone. Tracy could go home the following day. Before Emily walked back to the Y, she stopped at a pay phone and dialled Jimmy's number. Her despair had turned to a cool anger. A male voice answered the phone.

"Yeah?"

"Is this Jimmy?"

"Yeah, this is Jimmy. What do ya want?"

"This is Tracy's sister. I just wanted to tell you that you murdered your son. He just died because of you. How's it make you feel?"

Silence. Emily hung up and left for the Y, hoping there was enough beer in the sink to get drunk, to feel nothing.

The sisters took off to a small bar where Tracy often went. Emily found herself liking the country music as she danced around, nursing her beer, thinking, I've been in Winnipeg too long. I gotta get out of here. She watched her sister laugh with her friends and wondered if this was how Tracy dealt with all the horrors, shutting them out and talking as if nothing had happened, nothing was ever real. She wondered how her big sister lived, how she stayed in a relationship where she was being beaten. Did Tracy freeze as she did when she was a child?

Emily looked around the bar. Big burly men who looked like Manson wannabees. She wanted to get back to Montreal and decided to convince Tracy to leave with her.

After visiting the trailer that Tracy lived in, it didn't take much convincing. There was nothing for miles, except a creepy old man down the road. Cold white snow everywhere, bleak, barren. A lonely place. Poverty all around, dirt stains everywhere, no food or running water, no toilet, burns on the floor from the tiny wood stove. Mice crawled out of the holes. There wasn't much to pack or save. A shack filled with memories of beatings, memories of hunger. Sasha was dead.

Tracy was still sick and weak. All she had was an old rusty brown car. They had money enough to pay for gas, food, and stay in a motel room overnight. Emily had never driven in her life, but Tracy couldn't drive. Emily was willing to do anything to get Tracy out.

All Emily remembered of the drive was Wawa, eating white bread with SMUCKERS peanut butter and jelly, and singing *Lean on Me* with Tracy, their song during the long drive home. Only a miracle prevented Emily from crashing the car and killing them. Perhaps Sasha had something to do with that.

_____

A year later, Emily was living in Toronto. A call came in.

"Hi Em."

"Trace, how are ya, what you been up to?"

"I just wanted to call and tell you, Em, Jimmy died. He had a heart attack."

"He's dead?!!!" Emily cackled, disbelief and excitement shaping her voice. It was as if Tracy had told her she won the 6-49 lottery.

"Yeah, he's dead." Tracy needed to say it again, to make it true.

Emily felt good. She didn't tell Tracy how good she felt. Was there something wrong with feeling good about another human being's death? For a while she had wondered how calling him a murderer, the murderer of his son, affected him. But, it was the truth. A heart attack, at thirty-four. Emily hoped the truth had killed him. A little touch of justice.

"I love you Sasha," Emily whispered, closed her eyes and remembered him alive. His angel eyes.

Ruth Mandel

The Last Prayer

Each chunk we bite from life is a prayer. Our treasure chest homes,
our love-magnet pets, each meal
we grudgingly make and casually take.
Prayers to life
　　　let us flourish let us live
　　　let us stay leave us be let us stay leave us be.
Utterances we muster as we swallow, spurred by a rush,
gratitude and fear. Vehement pleas
　　　may we preserve what luck we have.

Babies are prayers. Mothering is prayer.
Each tasting kiss, each chattering
diaper change, each worn red sandal putting on　pulling off
each rambling invented story, each whispered
convincing promise. The cradles
we make of our voices, rocking　rocking
　　　may this remain just so may we all be here may we
　　　do this again and again and again tomorrow and for
　　　ever.

Each rolling, belly to belly nursing, a recitation.
Her milky new breath, when it collides
with mine, a sanctuary
between our mouths.
Our hands, as they flutter together
and apart. Our wondering fingers　together
and apart　uttering.

From the instant my doctor said, "Yes, finally,
you are pregnant" my hands
grafted themselves to my slow, anxious belly,
how my hands remained steadfastly there while my baby cracked through
me,
how my hands shifted to her setting head
        may we be safe may we be safe may we be safe
        may we be invulnerable.

The back of the hand faces outside: strategic armour.
The palm inside: devoted sentry.
Poised between the precious and the dangerous — between her head
and the table corner, her shoulders
and the stair she faces down, her eyes
and a violent sight.
The cradle
I make of my hands — infinite, furious,
futile.

        Those mothers, their babies,
        them too.

I know now what I was afraid of
trying to decide if we should have a child
what the ambivalence and fear warned
what those mothers knew
those mothers forced to stand, collapsing
in long, terrified lines.
My baby knows what their babies knew,
babies held in faltering arms, shielded
by mother's unyielding hand.

What is lighter than the mother's hand
What is heavier than the mother's exhausted arms
What is heavier than the baby urgent with need
The weight of your child.
The excessive, faultless pull of gravity, a downward
tug I never want to know; after the terrible trains, the father
gone, the baby in her arms for
ever.

And then in the gun point crush
the mother whispers, put your head on my shoulder.
Her hand cups the back of her baby's head,
her wrist at the nape of the neck, cradling.
Crushed in the chamber,
she draws the head inward,
interweaves shoulder chin cheek
tucks her nose into her baby's neck.
She inhales the tart,
moist scent that secrets there.
Her inhalation, a recitation. The rescuing breath,
held in her mouth.

Mothering, there.
Did she hold it deeply,
safely in her striving lungs.
Did she slowly exhale
close to her baby's mouth
a sanctuary.

In the terror of that leakless room, tugging
each other in the gas,
did she make a sudden choice, or
no choice. Instantaneous.

Later
those mothers, their babies,
extracted from the pile.
The mother's stiff, angled fingers
driven through her baby's
hard soft skull,
panic quickening.

The last protection,
not to suffer longer, not to be orphaned for an instant.
What those mothers suddenly knew
what they did. The fingers
loud and silent in their last plea. The hand's unbearable
story.
What they were so afraid of.
What we are so afraid of.
The last prayer.
The last mothering.

Henny Buncel

Silent Vigil

A soft, pervasive, morning dew floated.
Passing, I could smell the nasturtium as you smell them for
the first time
parfum enivrant
scent of dawn when a town is still asleep

I come back to these pleasure boats anchored at the foot of
Confederation Park. On this foggy morning, they float covered in
canvas ready for winter.
Silent vigil

At a distance, the ferry, *le traversier,* the *Upper Canada,*
inches smoothly to Wolfe Island.
I wait, wait, drowsy with the gulls
heads curled under wings, buried in feathers.
Out of time, in silent vigil
here and far away

In summer, these pleasure boats cruise the majestic St. Lawrence across
the Thousand Islands.
Hauntingly, I see those other boats that would drift in and
out of the harbor, being anchored and unloaded.

Boats in wartime France.

Again and again, we would come and stand, at a distance.
We watched.
On good days, we would actually sit on a rock nearby, making an ultimate claim on the action.
There was no action, or very little. A slow *va et vient.*
Fishing nets being repaired. Crates unloaded.
We watched in silent vigil.
Gulls on the alert for a hand-out.
They didn't seem to see us.
They were busy. They seemed to have a purpose in life.

We saw them — unloading, we saw them — loading.
They made no more sense to us than our invisible presence must have made to them. At times I would lie in the sun, doze off. As I woke another boat would slowly glide in. The skipper would yell to somebody at shore, *Attache moi.*

I would wonder if it was finally time for supper. Our time
to return to the group home, for some watery-milk, half-a-slice
of stale bread, on good days, half a baked potato.
Watching, I would rehearse how to say it, wonder what would
happen if I'd just say a simple sentence to one of those busy
guys.
"We are hungry"
"We are slowly starving"
"We are hungry all day long"

We never said anything. They must have known. We were those
refugee kids from the group home, in bathing suits with our
bloated stomachs and our long scrawny arms. Scavenger eyes.
From morning to dusk
Keeping vigil like the gulls.

The *Upper Canada* glides back, trailing a small jet of surf.

To my surprise, somebody else has sat down at the far end of
the bench. He looks like a "homeless" person, *un sans abri.* We
don't see as many here in Kingston as in Toronto. After eyeing
him from the back of my ears, I hear him say with a toothless
grin
"Warm enough for you"
I grumble "Yap, it's getting chilly "
He mutters "Been sleepin in a barn over on Lemoine's . . ."
I shake my head, pretend to be reading
He starts again "Been feeding them gulls . . ."
I lift my head this time, make some kind of fleeting eye contact, pick up the
book on my lap, wondering if I should change benches.
He must have read my thoughts, for he comes right out with it. "If you give
me a couple of loonies for a hot soup, I'll leave you alone ..."
I grab my purse, give him his money. He gets up immediately, shakes his
baseball cap, offers me another big toothless grin, and we wish each other,
"Have a good day."

I come back to this spot, like a knot in my guts, a real *noeud de vipère,* you could
say. Max Keeping reading the evening news bulletin, Haitians off the coast of
Florida are being sent back in U.S Patrol cruise boats to . . . In Ethiopia it is
estimated that 50% of the children under five years will die of starvation this
coming year if no relief is . . . a surplus in the potato crop of PEI may have
to be plowed back into the fields . . .
They call it "a problem of distribution." I know, our circuits are plugged,
bogged down with trivia, slush.
Immiscible static.
Poetry and prose don't mix. French and English, *God forbid,*
don't mix. Love and hate.
Hunger and food don't connect
The unspeakable gulf
Am I really part of this action, as I so demurely come back
to Confederation Park, to sit on a bench and watch boats load and
unload, in a world that makes no more sense to me then or now.

Jennifer Angold Morrow

Selling the House

Sky beguiles the eyes. Neither finite nor infinite, opaque nor transparent, ever since the Ice Age's thaw released people onto this earth, it has drawn the minds of young and old into questions as inscrutable as the phenomenon that creates its blue illusion. It changes vestments with the seasons; each robe reflects the many changing moods of its origin, the sun – pale in the morning, lustful in the afternoon, reluctant in the evening. Ten thousand blues. Yet for all its diversity it is a constant in our bewildering lives. Sky swallows time and engulfs distance. I can see a grandmother interrupt her long, painful walk across Spadina Avenue because only here can she see in the sky the hugeness that drew her child's eyes in Amdo province, eighty years ago. In fields all over the world, pouring from the exits of gold mines and coal mines, or pausing in photocopy rooms by the window, what labourer hasn't gazed heavenward to rest her eyes and still her mind? Sky gives license to freedom.

Late summer, twenty-six years old. I have climbed the flat roof to gaze at the sky unencumbered for the last time this season. The Sunday sounds of my Toronto street fall back behind leafy trees. My father's letter damp in my fingers. Brightness forces my eyes to close. The letter huge in crazy print. A light breeze breathes over me, blows away the soft smell of roof tar. The letter fades slightly. The silver maple stirs its leaves. When the wind settles I open my eyes to a squint. Almost clear. Over a base of sky I begin to chase dust across my pupils, up, then down, then up again, until I stop, frustrated. Shut my eyes. Orange flame. Open my eyes. Reach up to it.

This sky has followed me in flight; I turn to it to remember, send the fire of sight into its fire of light and a brighter sky blazes. This now, this is the sky only I have known. For vision is not merely a stream of light entering the eye; it occurs only when the eye reaches out to touch what it knows. It strokes the backs of its fingers along the cheek of a beloved's face, delves deep into the hold of memory to build into it everything that it has ever been. To see both past and present at once. So the eye creates the sky. And so I hold my breath, and fall in. From the sky of the present into the sky of memory, the scattering blue takes me to . . .

. . . a faraway suburb, where neat streets sleep on land that has given up its itch for corn. Memory clogs my senses. Cold weather snowsqueak melts to earth smell damply seeping from creases in fingers and hands. The smell of tar in August rises like the quivering heat haze; children play baseball at the end of the street. Kicking up crisp orange leaves from the piles at the edge of the road where you bury your friend or she buries you, better run now cause the poodle lady's going to yell. The trees have grown into themselves and their large August leaves confidently capture the open light around them. But they still whisper along the dusk wind, reach toward each other and rub boughs with a creak that wakens anxious children. The houses behind the trees are more comfortable as well. The area has become popular and the summers are filled with the sound of hammering and the smell of sawdust. Houses have widened from boxes to rectangles and decks, skylights, garages have appeared. Shrubs have grown up to mask shameful concrete foundations which sink into basements cut from a startled earth that only knew the whisper of plough.

If I walk along Dundonald Crescent, which isn't a crescent, I have to look to recognize all the houses, whose aluminum siding used to shine whitely, adolescent houses squinting under the skinny shadows of young trees. But they are still there. They look different but they're steeped in the memories of one, two, three generations, memories that reach into the mind's eye of those who may remember.

Late summer, six years old. I can hear the purr of cars, the click of heels, the squeak of springs in a baby carriage, the hollow bounce of a ball on pavement, the song of a starling in the trees. I can see Judy and Patty, sun-blond hair bristling out from elfin sun hats their mothers made from the same pattern. They're walking on either side of Anne, who's pushing a baby carriage. Judy insisting on pushing, reaches her hands up to the bar and wraps her fingers around it. Patty saying, It's my brother, I should push and besides I can reach better, and shows her. Anne saying, Hush Patty you'll wake your brother, and then Patty asks, Where's Clare today? Judy answers, In hospital – when we get home can we have some apple juice?

I can tell you something about every house I pass. That one. That's where they flooded the back yard every winter to make a skating rink. All the children were so jealous of the two French boys who lived there. And here, the Dobbs' house, a family of artists and boys. Bobby Dobbs was in my class, the only nice boy. In this house they gave out chocolate bars at Halloween, and next door, the Krause sisters wore the green tunics of the private school.

Turning the corner onto Glengarry Road, the piano teacher's house. Judy's and Patty's legs swing from the piano bench, skinny and chubby in turn, while their fingers stretch and stumble over wide keys. They're playing a duet, Patty's bass flawless, Judy's melody hesitant. Patty's blood sings soft and low and will find earthly reflection when she picks up her first cello at eight. Judy just feels sorry for the piano teacher who sighs and asks if she practised even once this week. Yes, Judy lies.

The red house on the corner. The Thompsons sold it and moved away fifteen years ago, and it's painted green now, but even today I shudder for all of the things I can't forget about Jimmy Thompson. Jimmy riding his bicycle in circles around Clare, calling her Retard and Loser, while she laughs and chases him, her sandals slap-slap-slapping on the pavement. Judy watching helpless as Jimmy's circle narrows around her sister, until he can touch her. He stops for a second and holds his hand on Clare's little chest. Clare standing still. Then he shoves her a little, wipes his hand on his jeans saying something about germs. Clare claps her hands and laughs as Jimmy rides off popping his gum. Seeing her little sister's tears Clare puts her arm awkwardly around Judy's shoulder wheezing,

"What's wong Baby? Baby do' cwy!"

Patty's house, warm and smelling of apple juice, with a little brother who was always there, and a fish tank with two goldfish the girls gazed at for hours. Mrs. Dorland's house with all the cats and, as Judy grew up and began to notice, antiquarian books and the septuagenarian's increasingly abstract oil paintings.

Aspen Avenue, which isn't an avenue. Judy's house. So like the others and so ungraspably different. The twin cedars standing guard outside the front door like red-coated soldiers at the Governor-General's house. Mummy's wild flowerbeds where violets, crocuses, lilies of the valley, irises, forsythia and small trees jostled for light beneath Miss Green's towering silver maples and Ernesto's apple trees. The vegetable garden's constant struggle against bugs, disease and rot. The swingset, the waterlogged ping pong table, the herb garden. My mother straightens from gardening and shades her eyes. I grab myself by the wrist to stop from running to her.

The ink from my father's letter stains my fingers. He writes, *This house is too big. I walk and hear my footsteps now. It is terrifying to follow only yourself, to be followed by your own feet only. Judy, I'm selling the house.*

The house I left ten years ago, ran away from full of dreams. I never noticed it squeezing into a dense decade of friends, books, lovers. I fought to earn my place on this city's streets. Paid the price of abandoned friendships, failed exams, eviction notices. This city builds its ghosts. Garrison Creek, Taddle Creek; blue gentians in High Park; whispers from the grave. Places in this city that draw me into memory even when I look away; Spadina Circle; Manning Avenue; the indistinct edge of Lake Ontario; the thousand banalities that make up a life's drama. I roam this city a proud queen, on foot or bicycle. Dark in the dark of night, a master of speed and direction. I know who drives the eight-fifteen Queen Streetcar on a summer night as the purple sky poses riddles above the Don River. But do I know how this city grieves? Does it long for the evening footfalls of the boys who sold the *Telegram*? Perhaps sometimes it twitches like Birchall's hanged limbs; perhaps that is what irks the sleepless. Can I trace shapes in the sidewalk cracks? Does Clare live here, outside of the photograph upon my desk? Does Pat matter at all? Does my mother dance in the dust shadows, in alleys she never trod?

Through the back door to the indoors, wood floors, home made apple juice popsicles, and the shapes of eccentric women peering from the bathroom linoleum. That door that never closed properly, the fluorescent tube that flickered until someone whacked it. The spot on the yellow carpet where Sweepy's catnip toy spilled one Christmas. Twenty years later, other cats would sniff the same ragged spot and scratch.

Clare's booster-chair is long-gone, in fact, there is little evidence of Clare beyond a framed photograph in my father's room; but as easily as August-hot pavement lifts to my nose or the crunching of leaves to my ears, my sister's face smiles from around every corner of this house. I can see her greeting Judy from her booster-chair when Judy got home from visiting Patty or walking round the pond. I can see the two little girls running round the backyard at a game of tag, Judy letting Clare catch her and then taking a long time to tag her back. It's August, grass is long as days. The girls run up and down the street with Patty, knee-skin grass-stain, in the sunshine in the rain. Dresses were made for removing and sprinklers to jump in and the three girls, bare-bum, jump in and out

again. Someone discovers it feels nice on her soo-soo place and someone's Mummy says it's not nice. On the next street the kids are at baseball. The girls might go join them later but for now there's grass to roll in
and summer's high and fine. Mummy's going to have another baby but
Judy doesn't know it yet. Grade one is about to begin but what does that
mean? All that matters is the certainty of sun and the length of evening
shadow, the sound of Mummy's voice when you need it.

From the piano teacher's house Debussy and Satie come to cool and
still a summer's eve, and in years to come Jude, lonely with a backyard
boyfriend, will hear cello from Pat's house and remember this evening.
This long hot summer that lasted forever, that spreads itself over my
memory with an insistence that can only come from the fall that followed. The summer before school started. Before Clare died. Before
Heather was born. Fresh tar, cut-grass, sandals whispering on pavement
because it was too hot to run and it was always time for a popsicle. There
are still children playing ball up the street, quivering behind the haze,
and I am drawn to look up into the wide clear sky as the people I loved
fall away, as the suburb returns to farm, farm returns to forest, forest is
crushed under the weight of ice moving south into a time before anyone
dreamed of sky.

mariko tamaki

A Stalking Story

A stocking: a long sock which briefly clings to the upper thigh only to
sink down around the knees when walking commences.
A stalking: a set path of potential interception; a prolonged near
miss.

July 4th: *Last night I stood outside her house, hidden amongst
the trees and bushes, barely breathing. Tangled in her tree line, I
watched her lights go out one by one until the house was a sleeping giant with all eyes closed. I stood in the brush for two hours,
barely breathing, while tiny insects made their way up my stock-
ings. She read herself to sleep by what looked like the glow of a
lantern, sitting by the window, her bent silhouette like something
you would see in a child's storybook. At 12:30 am, she shut her
book and clicked off the last light. It was strangely calming to
know she was asleep, asleep with me so close and yet so uninvited.
Sweet dreams. When all the lights were out, I snuck, twig by twig,
branch by branch, back to my car, parked several blocks away.
Noting the numerous bites on my calves, I decided a better stalker
would acquire some sort of insect repellent.*

I am not alone. Two years ago at University in Montreal my roommate,
Katie, spent an entire semester stalking a red-headed boy named Julian
who sat two rows ahead of her in American Poetry. Within three weeks
she knew not only his name and student number (9345672 – copied off
his Whitman exam), but also where he lived (2348 St. Urbain), with whom
he lived (a guy named John, an ugly guy named Stan, and a cat named
Smoke) his phone number (849-6268) and his fall schedule (mostly boring poetry classes). For months we (because she needed an accomplice)
would bus halfway across town to have coffee in this smoky little Italian
place which happened to be not only outrageously expensive, but also

two blocks away from where Julian lived. Sipping sour espressos we would anxiously sit and smoke, chatting in hushed tones, our voices poking through the clouds of cigarette fumes hanging between us.

"I dream about him," Katie confessed one day, near the end of this particular obsession.

"I dream about him. Sometimes in my dreams you and I are sitting down for coffee and he comes in and sits down with us and puts his hand on my knee. He leans forward to whisper something into my ear, something soft and not so important, and I can smell his neck. That mix of old spice and the smell of an old cottage right after it rains, I wake up and I can still smell it. Like he's actually been there."

Only dreams.

Why is it so hard to believe that?

Memory Log: The Scene: *I am sitting on a grassy hill in Eglinton Park while she runs back to her car to retrieve a present left under the front seat. The sun filters through the trees and I am dappled white and grey. The taste of sticky grapefruit lingers in my mouth and welds my fingers together. Already I am imprinted with the shape of her chin, once resting on my shoulder, already I miss her and imagine she will never return from the car, that she will jump in her silver bug and drive away and that I will never see her again. Ever. When she returns, she kneels in front of me and makes me guess which hand conceals her treasure. A hand creeps into my hair as she pulls out my prize: smooth, round, orange, Greek worry beads. "Pour VOUS . . ." she says "p o u r   v o u s . . ."*

Over and over.

Smooth orange beads absorbing the heat of the sun,

little metal links burning my palm.

And then I wake up.

But she's not just a dream, I tell myself, she's more. It's only NOW that she's stuck in my dreams, once she was a real living creature in my life. I KNOW her, I tell myself, I know her. This is not a dream.

I can only wonder what Katie would say if she saw me skulking back to my Honda at 12:36 a.m. Was it not I who condemned her similar hobby as both ridiculous and possibly dangerous? "You could be arrested," I

told her when I caught her with a photocopy of one of his term papers, though I was not, admittedly, sure if this was true. This is possibly an avenue, now, worth investigating. Certainly, if not a criminal, I am at least a liar, telling my mother I am out meeting friends for coffee, fortunate that she never asks me with WHOM or WHERE I am going.
"Mum, I am going to stalk my former English teacher, whom, you may or may not recall, was the woman who stole my heart."

6 years ago.

Memory Log: Grade 11, English class, Shakespeare
Romeo: [To Juliet.] *If I profane with my unworthiest hand*
     This holy shrine, the gentle fine is this:
     My lips, two blushing pilgrims, ready stand
     To smooth that rough touch with a tender kiss.
Juliet: *Good pilgrim, you do wrong your hand too much,*
     Which mannerly devotion shows in this;
     For saints have hands that pilgrims hands do touch,
     And palm to palm is holy palmers' kiss.
She crouched down by my desk and entwined her slender fingers in my open hand. "O, then, dear saint, let lips do what hands do" It bugs me to think that such a moment could have merely been a class demonstration and not a genuine sign of affection. I blushed. Didn't Juliet? She smiled . . . and kissed him. I would clip that moment out of time with a pair of sewing scissors and tuck it in my wallet if I could. IF I could.

It is hard to have to remind myself that I am not Romeo, nor am I Robin Hood or Joan of Arc or any other romantic hero-ine. Harder to have to remind myself that what I am doing, my stalking, is neither romantic nor adventurous (nor, I suspect, even flattering) only slightly strange and perhaps misguided, the act of a bored university student who is wasting her summer vacation living off her parents; eating chips and watching late nite TV.
Nonetheless, I pen the word "STALKER" on my left hand. Every time the ink fades I re-ink it, so that soon it gains the standing of a sort of semi-permanent tattoo, ingrained in the microscopic creases of my epidermis. Whenever someone asks me about it, I say it is a note to myself to remind me to rent this student film I want to see. "A reminder to do . . ."

130

TO DO
1. Drive by her house again.
2. Call her answering machine and hang up.
3. See shrink.

A friend tells me the story of this friend of a friend who was caught stalking when she called this guy something like 20 times only to be nabbed the 21st time when the enraged stalkee picked up the phone and screamed "WHO THE FUCK IS THIS?!" "Oh hi," the stalker fibbed, "I'm sorry. . . . . is this Amelio's Pizza?"

"YOU HAVE BEEN CALLING ALL DAY!" The guy screamed, "Who is this anyway? 246-4345? (stalker's number!!) This isn't Julie is it?"

This was during the advent of that modern telephone feature we now call CALL DISPLAY, a technological breakthrough good for avoiding parents' calls, but a notorious thorn in the stalker's side. Funny, but also a reminder to think ahead. Don't want to get caught by a lousy BELL Telephone service. I revise my list.

4. Buy calling card to make all calls
   from pay phones around the city.
5. Buy chalk.

I decide to up the ante.

I think, I tell myself, that I want her back. If this is true, stalking is a questionable solution. Stalking, after all, is one-sided. It is also, undoubtedly, a pursuit without a definite goal, unlike the hunt, where the ultimate goal is to claim your prey by capturing it or killing it. BANG. Stalking is all about watching and waiting. Ultimately, a stalker must ask herself, what am I waiting for? Confrontation . . .

A coward's confrontation.

A message.

I deliberate for several hours over my message, which I decide will be written in chalk rather than spray paint because it's cheaper and less damaging. I consider quoting a bible or Shakespearean verse but in the end decide that is too pretentious. I plan to write:

ABANDONED ?

I'm counting on the fact that I am special, that I am, in other words, the only little girl whose heart she ever broke.

It never even occurs to me that I could be wrong.

July 10th: *Creeping out from behind a particularly prickly pine I pulled a piece of chalk from the box with a shaky hand. The ground hummed with quiet. A jury of sleepy houses watched my movements as I crossed the lawn, step by inching step, and stood in front of her porch, listening with every fibre in my body for that one sound, a creak or a whisper, that would send me flying for my car. My blood rushed like an arctic waterslide through my veins. My mouth went dry. The chalk made more noise than I had planned. I guess my porch at home was more solid, maybe a little newer. I ended up writing something longer too, though I cannot completely explain why I wrote what I did.*

WHAT
was
i
to
YOU ?

I fled the scene as soon as I had dotted my question mark. I ran. I ran like a cat with its tail on fire, like a sprinter bounding out of the blocks. I held my tears, like a runner balancing an egg in an egg-spoon race, till I got to the car. Then, tired, I let my tears fall. I dropped my keys on the sidewalk, tucked my feet under the car and leaned my head on the door, the cold surface soon warm with the heat of my tears. It was almost ten minutes before I could drive home. I went home by a different route, a longer route, that took me past my old school. I stopped by the little park by my house for a smoke before going home.

Of course I left the chalk, the incriminating evidence, on the porch, though I only realized that when I went to grab a cigarette from my pocket and noticed I wasn't holding anything in my hand. Could chalk be fingerprinted? WOULD it be fingerprinted?

Probably not.

The next day, however, I spend my hours a fugitive around a neighbours'
pool, hiding behind a pair of my mom's Jackie O's and a book on Nixon
I'm not really reading. Stress and suspense eat away at my stomach like a
bad veggie lasagna. Yuck. When a friend calls to ask me out for a coffee
("Care for a little espresso?") I'm dressed and out the door before she can
even hang up.
"You look nervous," my friend says, "Are you okay?"
"Just tired."
"Too many late nights?"
"Sort of."
"You know, you should really use your spare time, you know, while you
still have it. Like, a hobby or something. I mean, next summer you're
going to have a ton of work, especially since you'll be moving and every-
thing."
"Any suggestions?"
"Oh, shit, I don't know. Pottery."
Pottery.
Hmmmm . . .

TO DO
1. ~~Drive by her house again.~~
2. ~~Call her answering machine and hang up.~~
3. ~~See shrink.~~
4. ~~Buy calling card to make all calls from pay phones around the city.~~
5. ~~Buy chalk.~~
6. Take up pottery.
7. See shrink.

I drive by her house after coffee. A bucket of water with a rag draped over
the rim sits by the door. Parked several blocks away, I return biting my
top lip and clenching my fists. An answer, not clearly visible from the

street or the sidewalk, is scrawled over the grey smear of what was left of my previous message.

An answer. And a question.

WHO ARE YOU ?

For the second time in the past week I run until my lungs feel like they're going to burst out of my body and lunge ahead of me. This time, however, I do NOT cry. I drive home. Have a cigarette. Feel nothing.

That night, I try to imagine what she must have looked like discovering my message the previous morning. Virtual stalking. I know she usually has a tea and reads the paper in the morning, I imagine the paper would have landed somewhere on the message. Did she stop, when she saw it, walk down the steps (careful to avoid the writing) and stare? Did a hand make its way to gaping mouth? Did her hands shake as mine had as she went to retrieve a bucket of warm water and soap to scrub away my scrawl?

Did she know it was me?

She said she knew me.

"I know you," she told me, sitting next to me on the bed and stroking my hair as I fumbled with the book on my lap.

"I know you know me."

It seemed to be true.

But if it was true, did she know that with every touch, with every sigh and every kiss on my forehead, that I was reeling? Did she know, that in addition to making my life easier, in addition to saving my life (as I have always said she did) she was also tearing it apart?

> **Memory Log: The scene:** *[Long before the orange beads burned into my palm] I am sitting in a chair crying. My entire body is wet with tears and heavy with grief. Everything is about to end: school, class, her. She is leaving. But before she leaves, off to Thailand, she sits opposite me in a similar chair and stares at me. She doesn't*

believe me. I've told her I can't take it anymore. I, for the first time, believe me; I believe (I know) it is OVER. I feel a darkness seeping up from the floor and into my shoes, feel it pulling at the back of my neck. I sob. She stands. She puts her arms around me and tells me she will never, EVER, let go. "You're mine now," she tells me. It seemed to be true.

Was it?
I don't know what I want.
I want it to be settled. I want it to settle, so that when it comes up in my dreams I can awake the next morning and not want it to be, not think it is, real. I am tired of near misses, of close encounters, of memories, and watching. I am a crappy stalker.

July 13th: *I waited a while before returning. I took the subway to her house and walked. It took longer to get there than I thought, so it was late when I got there, but not as late as usual. The house was dark and quiet. No reading, I guessed, tonight. I pulled the piece of chalk from my pocket and tip-toed up the walkway.*

SORRY

I wrote

GOOD BYE

I wrote it and meant it. I turned back, taking the chalk with me, and headed home.

I
have
not
returned.

For R.C. and T.L.

She's...

Lisa Ayuso is an ass-kickin', wannabe rockstar who is currently co-ordinating the revolution of revolutions. Formerly an underground French spy, Lisa is now running Heartbreaker zine distribution and is in the process of publishing both Fat Chance #2 and the first issue of Oh Me, Oh My.

Sharon Baltman: I am an M.D. Psychotherapist working in downtown Toronto. I began writing while living on a kibbutz for a year in Israel five years ago. When I started being a serious passenger on a motorcycle in 1995, I hadn't been on a motorcycle since age 18. I live in Toronto with my 16-year-old daughter, Arielle.

brenda brown is a writer, artist and psychotherapist who is mostly con-sumed with her project, "Forbidden Expressions: Lost Bodies & Wild Imaginations", which explores artful telling practices. She is living unabandoned in collaboration with Robin, Sassafras and Sequoia. She has been previously published in *Contemporary Verse 2* under the pseu-donym "brass".

Henny Buncel lives part-time in Kingston, part-time in Toronto. She has been published in *Breaking the Chain, Fireweed, Textual Studies*. She is currently the editor of a local newsletter. She is looking forward to being a grandmother for the first time, in the meanwhile she is in the process of bonding with her computer.

Sherree Clark: I've come full circle in my life. As a young girl I wanted to be a writer as well as an artist, but while in University I switched to Psychology. Then I became a teacher and later a Child & Play Therapist. Now I'm back to writing and drawing and appreciating the time I have to explore my first loves and dreams all over again.

Lesley Anne Cowan is a secondary school teacher and writer living in Toronto. She is working on her first collection of short stories.

Leah Darke is a wannabe Toronto writer and office drudge. She occasion-ally contributes to *Siren* Magazine and *Gaywire* on CIUT radio, when she's not geekin' on the net.

Ann Decter is a novelist, editor and publisher. Author of two novels, *Honour* and *Paper, Scissors, Rock*, Ann spent five years as co-managing editor at Women's Press in Toronto and is co-founder and publisher of McGilligan Books. She gets her kicks raising Rosie, writing, and supporting other women to develop as writers.

Rosamund Elwin has dreams of publishing a full novel. She has published short stories and poems in *No More Masterpieces, Diva, At the Crossroads, Getting Wet, Tangled Sheets* and other publications she can't remember. She is the author of *Asha's Mums* and *The Moonlight Hide and Seek Club*.

S.P. Larade is a an archivist and choral singer who touched down in Toronto twelve years ago. She has been writing stories since grade two when *The Adventures of Googie* chronicled her travels as a military brat.

Ruth Mandel: I have just completed my first poetry manuscript, *How To Tell Your Children About the Holocaust*. I have had poems published in *Prairie Fire, The Fiddlehead, The Antigonish Review, Parchment, Contemporary Verse 2, Fireweed* and *Canadian Woman Studies*, and in the anthology *Vintage 97/98*. Raising my daughter and our two dogs with my partner in this our world is my continuous poetic and brave endeavour.

Annie Coyle Martin was born in Ireland and came to Canada when she was twenty-one. She has been making up stories for over fifty years. She lives in Toronto and has four children and two grandchildren.

Jennifer Angold Morrow is a social and environmental activist and writer. She lives in Toronto, a city she loves.

Monica Noy a.k.a. Bitch Queen From Hell (BQFH); the Red-crested Australian Nordle Beast or the almost forgotten femmo, leso, pinko, greenie bastard. An apsiring writer, deep undercover. Last seen dressed conservatively in the downtown financial district having a bevy with known members of the old boys club. She is known to be armed with an overused and somewhat pretentious literary theory vocabulary and is not afraid to deconstruct.

Kari Reynolds fuses commitment to social justice with a sense of adventure. Her current manuscript includes unusual stories from her volunteer work with Innu, indigenous people of Labrador and eastern Quebec. Kari has joined protest camps in a bombing range and a new mining development. She has been overflown by NATO jets, arrested and jailed alongside Innu. Her story in this anthology takes place in the relative safety of the village of Sheshatshiu.

Sharon Rosenberg, Ph.D., is a teacher and an editor with a passion for writing. She has taught courses in Canadian women's fiction, gender and sexuality and contemporary feminist theory and activism. A current project is the creation of a poetry manuscript on the intersection between memory and desire.

Elizabeth Ruth is a 30-year-old writer and editor who has moved 51 times, loves any cover of the song *Wild World*. Under a psuedonym she has a 9 to 5 life - a figment of someone else's imagination. Elizabeth values passion over stability and risk over safety, which may explain why she is working on a collection of related short stories and her first novel.

Shlomit Segal is an artist and writer whose fabric work was featured in Toronto's Mayworks, 1998. A member of the editorial collective of the Jewish feminist journal *Bridges*, Shlomit is a long-time activist on feminist, class and progressive Jewish issues and a former printer with the *Our Times* worker co-operative.

Noreen Shanahan: From a background in feminist journalism, I shifted into poetry a year or so ago and now feel a slide into prose. Meanwhile, I remain firmly planted in and thoroughly dedicated to all my daily diaries. I realize, simply put, that writing is breath for me.

mariko tamaki is 22. She thinks her dreams are important and writes them all down. mariko would be nothing if I weren't for her psychologist and her English Teachers who have supported her with their persistence and willingness to listen to her dreams. Maybe, if mariko is lucky, she will grow up and be a writer.

Joanne Vannicola: All my life I have made the words of other writers come to life in movies, on TV and on stage, as an actor. For a few years I have been secretly working on voicing my own words on the page. Who knows what the future may bring. I am currently working on an anthology for women on health, and slowly working on a personal/political non-fiction novel.

Zoe Whittall is a sweet talkin' teleresearcher, and ex-farm girl. She has been published in *Fireweed, Flux* magazine and *Index*, as well as the many pocket-sized *'zines* she has created.

Karen Woodman contributed to *Queer View Mirror 2*. She wrote a column for the *Dawson City Insider* and now lives in Toronto. She studied fine art at the Emily Carr Institute of Art and Design.

Mehri Yalfani was born in Hamadan, Iran. After high school she moved to Tehran to study. She graduated from University of Tehran in electrical engineering. In 1987, she immigrated to Canada. She has published seven books, three collections of short stories and three novels in Farsi, her mother language, and a collection of short stories and poems, *Parastoo*, in English. Her works have appeared in *Fireweed* and *Dandelion*, as well.

Acknowledgments

She's Gonna Be is one of those rare projects that is pure chemistry. A chance remark at the right the moment, and suddenly all you can see is that it is, really, possible. To that first voice that said, "why don't we do a little book of our writing?" and to each of the women whose writing is published in this book, a sweet rain barrel of thanks for the ignition, the fuel, the timing and that spark — belief.

From one a title, from another, a cover, from a third, the hours and hours it takes to turn pages of writing into pages for a book. And a forth and a fifth, and. . . mariko tamaki said "She's gonna be famous," and from that, a dozen or so of us carved a title. Snatchwear purveyor and lit organizer Beth Pettigrew did the copy edit, and Noreen Shanahan, thoroughly and carefully, the proof, while I vacationed. Advice and aesthetics came from Heather Guylar and Shlomit Segal and Ruthie Mandel. And thanks, Jennifer for your finely-honed reading

sherree clark turned a slide from Leah Decter's *romantic notions* installation into this happening cover, one rose at a time. Romantic notions indeed. Leah, thanks for the long distance art and for so much more. Keep that candle burning bright.

Women's Press gave us access to space and to a slowly greening computer for layout, where Karen Woodman spent far too many patient hours, checking fonts and spaces, word by word, line by line. She's that someone it wouldn't have been possible without. Thanks for giving us so much of June, Karen. Watch out for those night-flying birds.

I've been singing a new-old tune lately ♪♪ *make something happen, make just one something happen* ♪♪ Geno, thanks for accepting that more often than not I'd still rather make something happen than make a buck. And to Michael, for seeing that this is me.

This is the first all-girl — do we get to be kick-ass women again soon? — production from McGilligan Books, and it's here because of everyone who believed it could be. Write on.

Ann Decter